Watchwords Volume II
Words That Transform the Soul

by

Roger C. Bethel

Author's Tranquility Press
Marietta, Georgia

Roger C. Bethel/Author's Tranquility Press
2706 Station Club Drive SW
Marietta, GA 30060
www.authorstranquilitypress.com

Publisher's Note: This is a work of non-fiction.

Ordering Information:
Quantity sales. Special discounts are available on quantity purchases by corporations, associations, and others. For details, contact the "Special Sales Department" at the address above.

Watchwords Volume II/Roger C. Bethel
Paperback: 978-1-957208-30-5
eBook: 978-1-957208-31-2

Scripture quotations marked KJV are from the Holy Bible, King James Version (Authorized Version). First published in 1611. Quoted from the KJV Classic Reference Bible, Copyright © 1983 by The Zondervan Corporation.

Table of Contents

Introduction

Watchwords That Transform the Soul

Romans 12:1-2 (KJV)

The words in this devotional are a collection of simple terms from the Bible that I share with a daily telephone prayer line called Transformation Prayer Ministry (TPM). I co-host this prayer line with my wife, Viola, Mondays through Fridays.

When I began sharing a word each day, I would pray and ask God what he wanted to share at the end of the prayer conference call. Often, I would get a leading in my spirit of the word he wanted me to talk about. Other times I would hear a word in a sermon or during my daily meditation, and it would leap out at me in my mind. Sometimes, I would ask God over and over if that was the word he wanted to share with us. However, sooner or later, I'd have to just trust him and come to a conclusion.

I was always led to share on a level where, hopefully, everyone would understand and would be inspired. As you will notice, many of the devotionals consist of my personal stories that I hope will relate to others.

As you read through and meditate on each word, I encourage you to look for the subtle wisdom in the Southern conversational tone. Most of all, I pray you will be blessed and inspired.

The words used in this book are derived from various versions of the Holy Bible including the King James Version (KJV), New King James Version (NKJV), New International Version (NIV), New Living Translation (NTL), Amplified Bible (AMP).

Watchwords II

Words That Transform the Soul

Transformation

A gradual change in the form, behavior, and appearance of a person, place, or object.

"And be not conformed to this world: but be ye transformed by the renewing of your mind, that ye may prove what is that good, and acceptable, and perfect, will of God." Romans 12:2 (KJV)

As we look at the word "transformation" taken from Romans 12 verse 2, it says be not conformed to this world but be transformed by the renewing of your mind so that you can prove what is that good and acceptable and perfect will of God. Notice, there are three phases of transformation in the sight of God.

First, the good will; secondly, the acceptable will; and thirdly the perfect will of God. The transformation process for Christians is not a one-time event, but a lifelong journey.

It starts with the new birth experience with the good will of God for us. That's when God rescues us from the grips of Satan and restores us into the likeness of his image as he created us in the beginning, even before our foreparents sold us out in the Garden of Eden.

Then the process of transformation continues throughout our earthly journey of life. Again, starting with the new birth experience, which is also referred to as the born-again experience, it's a new beginning that changes us from an old, unregenerate, natural person the way we came out of our mother's womb. The new birth lays the foundation for the transformation process.

The word "transformation" is derived from the English word, metamorphosis, which means to change in stages. Transformation is just the opposite of complacency. I've heard people say, "I've been this way all my life and I ain't about to change."

You know what Jesus said about the Pharisees and Sadducees who refused to listen to him so they could be changed. He said, *"By your traditions you have made the word of God of no effect." Matthew 15:6 (KJV).*

Every day we have to be willing and obedient to go higher in the Word of God.

As mentioned earlier, the best example I can find for the transformation process is the word "metamorphosis."

The three stages of metamorphosis the butterfly goes through before reaching maturity include: 1) it starts off as an egg or larvae, 2) it starts crawling around as a caterpillar, and then 3) it begins to hang out as a chrysalis in preparation for flight. The final stage is a beautiful four-winged creature that gets up off the leaves and begins to fly. We don't normally see butterflies crawling around after they've finished eating. They do what they were created to do…and that's fly.

Now that's exactly how God created us to be as Christians who have become born-again into God's good will and who learn how to crawl our way through and be transformed into his acceptable will.

At that point we begin to shed off the scales of a worm and begin to fly and soar over the obstacles that block our progress.

To illustrate the perfect will of God is the third stage in the transformation process of the butterfly, where it is nestled in chrysalis, preparing to take flight.

Because of human abuse of God's most prized creation (mankind), the manufacturer had to make a mass recall for all humans to be *born again*, recreated, refinished into God's image, and relabeled as sons and daughters of God. While God is doing his work in us, he is preparing us to fulfill his purpose for us. Of course the transformation is a lifelong process, but he gives us what we need when we need it to accomplish his will.

Jesus said in John 3:3 (KJV), *"Except a man be born again, he cannot see the kingdom of God."* God could not put his brand, his stamp of approval as a brand new product on the Earth until he sent his Son to come down from heaven and re-create us into a new creature.

The late Dr. Myles Munroe said it like this: "The new birth is total recall from the manufacturer." After God the Father saw gross malfunctions in the human race, of no fault of his own, but due to misuse and abuse of privilege, he sent out a recall on all humans. He had to recreate us back into our original image.

Let's back up for just a second to remind you that the first humans, Adam and Eve, lost their image to the stain of sin by disobeying God. He then had to send a second Adam to restore us back into the likeness of the Godhead of the Father, Son and Holy Spirit with a new birth. He actually re-made us into a new spiritual creation. Again, God stamps his approval on us by rebranding us with the image of his only begotten Son, Jesus, the Christ. 2 Corinthians 5:17 (KJV) says, *"Therefore if any man be in Christ, he is a new creature; old things are passed away; behold, all things are become new."* We then have to learn the principles of God, as Isaiah 28:10 (KJV) says: *"Precept upon precept, line upon line, here a little and there a little."* All the preceding is being done as we go through the transformation process into God's perfect will.

All of this is done because of God's perfect desire for us as expressed in 3 John 1:2 (KJV), which says, *"Beloved, I wish above all things that thou mayest prosper and be in health, even as thy soul prospereth."* So, to the same degree and in the same manner as our soul prospers, God wants us to do well in every other area of our lives. In essence, I believe III John 1:2 tells us that God wants us to be healthy and happy even while we're on our way to heaven.

Prayer

Heavenly Father, in the name of Jesus, I thank you for your living word and the desire you have put in my heart to be transformed by the renewing of my mind. I ask you to convict me every time I am tempted to commit sin that crucifies Jesus afresh. I thank you for making a way of escape from every temptation I am confronted with. In Jesus' precious name I pray. Amen!

Accusation

Accusation is one of the enemy's weapons of choice to get the upper hand on believers in Christ.

"And I heard a loud voice saying in heaven, Now is come salvation, and strength, and the kingdom of our God, and the power of his Christ: for the accuser of our brethren is cast down, which accused them before our God day and night."
Revelation 12:10 (KJV)

Have you ever been falsely accused? If so, you know how it feels. And it's one thing to be falsely accused, but it's a whole other thing for people to believe the lie. Sometimes we may be falsely accused, and at other times we may be guilty of the accusation.

The father of accusations is the "father of lies and deception," known as Satan.

"And the great dragon was cast out, that old serpent, called the Devil, and Satan, which deceiveth the whole world: he was cast out into the earth, and his angels were cast out with him."Revelation 12:9 (KJV)

As long as we live, we will face accusations. But to be falsely accused is an injustice instigated by the devil—as falsely accusing Christians is one of Satan's primary jobs on Earth.

"Accusation" is the act of attributing blame for

wrongdoing. Accusation is one of the enemy's weapons of choice to get the upper hand on us . . . to disturb our peace of mind; to undermine our purpose and destroy our faith.

The text says, *"And the great dragon was cast out, that old serpent, called the Devil and Satan, which deceiveth the whole world; he was cast out into the earth, and his angels were cast out with him." Revelation 12:9 (KJV.)*

Get this— the accuser was cast out into the Earth. Reading that scripture you can see why so many are *"catching the devil"* so to speak.

If you've been falsely accused, you've experienced how it challenges your faith, but being accused when you're guilty can make you feel bad, too. Yet God gives us hope. He says that we who are guilty, have an advocate before the judge. If God has recently blessed you, then Satan has or will falsely accuse you.

Let's look at verse 10 again:

"And I heard a loud voice saying in heaven, Now is come salvation, and strength, and the kingdom of our God, and the power of his Christ, for the accuser of our brethren . . . which accused them before our God, day and night." Revelation 12:10 (KJV)

And here's the good news:

"And they overcame him by the blood of the Lamb and by the 'word of their testimony...'" Revelation 12:11 (KJV)

Glory to our God and Lord, Jesus Christ! Whenever

falsely accused, you can win your case by the word of your testimony.

What is the word of your testimony? We can answer that with another question . . . Who is the Word? Revelation 19:13 (KJV) says, *"His Name is called the Word of God."* That's Jesus, the Christ!

Wherever the people of God show up, you can be sure Satan will be there. Check out this Biblical example:

"One day the angels came to present themselves before the Lord and Satan also came with them." Job 1:6 (NIV)

When one of the pastors has backslidden, and time comes to elect the new pastor, the accuser of the brother shows up at the church meeting, doesn't he? I've seen this happen time and time again.

In conclusion, we are told by God to watch and pray. Stay sober (alert) and vigilant because the adversary is always walking about seeking if he can find something to falsely accuse you of before God.

Prayer

Father, in the name of Jesus, I thank you for giving us the strength to endure any accusation that may or may not be true. You said we are more than conquerors, and that no weapon formed against us shall prosper.

In spite of the false accusations made against us, we are victors, not victims. Thank you, Father, for being our advocate. In Jesus' name, Amen!

Authority

Authority is given to believers to take dominion over the Earth.

"Behold I give you the authority to trample on serpents and scorpions, and over all the power of the enemy, and nothing shall by any means hurt you."Luke 10:19 (NKJV)

The word for today is "authority." This authority is a gift from Jesus to those who believe in him.

The dictionary says authority is a lawful right and power to enforce obedience. The word, "authority" is a very distinct principle in biblical language. Authority of believers in Christ Jesus is delegated by God the Father.

Sometimes I wonder if we, as believers, really realize the authority we have on Earth. Just think about it, Jesus shared this with his disciples even before they received the baptism of the Holy Ghost.

The English origin of the word is author. Author is the originator or creator of a work or project.

The believer's authority comes from Jesus who happens to be the originator and final authority of our faith according to Hebrews 12:2(a) (KJV), *"looking unto Jesus, the author and finisher of our faith..."*

There are all kinds of authority. We have governmental authority; authority in the home; and authority in the workplace, to name a few. But regardless of who the earthly liaison is, in essence, all authority originates with God, the creator, and he expects us to adhere.

I think the most profound and imperative type of authority is the authority of the believer in Christ Jesus. This type of authority is specifically designed to maintain control and dominion in the Earth over demonic activity.

This authority is royal! Its diplomatic authority that's delegated from heaven where all the rules and regulations are grounded and rooted in the Word of God, forever settled.

It's the same authority God gave mankind when he created him in his own likeness and image. But the creature, man, failed to exercise his proper authority over Satan, and that failure has been following mankind ever since. That failure came about because of doubt that came through deception.

You see, the serpent, which represented the adversary to God's creation, twisted God's words and deceived the woman. The woman enticed the man, and they both disobeyed God's commandment. Ever since then, mankind has had the tendency to follow a pattern of deception, doubt, and unbelief.

I believe that's one of the main reasons so many Christians allow Satan to run rough-shod all over them.

It is my opinion that too many Christians don't really believe the authenticity of Luke 1:19 when Jesus says that believers in him have authority over serpents and *"over all power of the enemy and NOTHING by any means shall hurt you."*

That means sickness, poverty, iniquity, fear, doubt, confusion, anxiety, depression…nothing, which means NO THING, by any means, shall hurt you.

Hey, we've got to remember we are ambassadors of Christ with delegated authority from heaven in earthly affairs according to the Word of God. That literally means that any time something is not right in our domain, we should speak directly to God, our heavenly commander about it.

The Bible says in 1 Corinthians 14:2 that we, through the Holy Spirit, can speak directly to God about any issue that challenges us on the Earth. When we allow the Holy Spirit to give the words and we give it the voice, no man understands us, not even ourselves because we are speaking mysteries to God as the Holy Spirit gives us the language to which we give sound.

After studying Jude 1:20, I firmly believe when we talk to God in the Spirit, we actually build up ourselves to receive revelation knowledge, spiritual understanding, and wisdom from God, the Father. Therefore, anything contrary to the will of God that comes against us, any tormentor—anything that doesn't line up with the Word of God—we have authority over it.

All we have to do is do what Jesus did on the Mount of Temptation. Just say, "It is written." I believe as it is written in Romans 8:37 we are more than a conqueror; no lie, no deception the enemy forms against us shall prosper because my Father, God, says we are like a tree planted by the rivers of water and whatever we do will prosper.

Saints of God, you and I, as believers have the authority in our mouths. Proverbs 18:21 says death and life are in the power of the tongue.

If Eve, in the Garden of Eden, had addressed Satan like Jesus did, Jesus would not have had to go to the cross to save us from defeat on earth and eternal death. Sin wouldn't have entered the Earth's realm. All she had to do was submit to God, resist the devil, and he would flee, according to James 4:7. The same holds true for us today.

A believer's spiritual authority works just like a uniformed police officer's authority; it works in the natural, only better.

When we see a police officer's badge or even a blue light flashing behind us while we are driving, we quickly "straighten up and fly right," so to speak. If the officer pulls us over and flashes that badge, we don't have any problem obeying his authority. If he tells us to get out of the car, nine times out of ten we're going to obey.

It's the same way with our spiritual authority if we use it with the confidence of God's Word backing us up. The enemy is going to back down and obey.

We as Christians are ambassadors of heaven operating with seven spiritual weapons: 1) the helmet of salvation, 2) the breastplate of righteousness, 3) the belt of truth, 4) the shoes of peace, 5) the sword of the Spirit, 6) the shield of faith, and 7) the shoes of peace and tank of prayer. (Ephesians 6:14-18, paraphrased)

I believe God wants us to be like Jesus, the Apostle Paul, and Peter when they laid their hands on the crippled, blind, and sick folks, and the evil spirits loosed them, and they were restored.

I believe God is still in the business of restoring his people, and he has given us the authority to take back his kingdom by force as expressed in Matthew 11:12.

Prayer

Father, in the name of Jesus, we thank you that you have equipped us as believers with the authority and power to lay hands on the sick and cast out evil spirits.

Heavenly Father, we ask you to help us in our unbelief.

Father, we want to fulfill the commission you have delegated to us.

We want to be productive on Earth as we occupy it until Jesus returns and to hear him say, "Well done my good and faithful servant."

Thank you, Lord! We believe that we receive, even now, as we pray. Amen!

Certain

Sure of my relationship with God.

"Having carefully investigated everything from the beginning, I also have decided to write an accurate account for you, most honorable Theophilus, so you can be certain of the truth of everything you were taught." Luke 1:3-4 (NLT)

The word for today is "certain."

First of all, I want to ask a rhetorical question, just answer it in your heart: Are you certain that Jesus Christ is the only begotten Son of God; that he was conceived without an earthly biological father, that he was born to a natural born earthly woman?

Now consider these questions:

- Are you certain that Jesus is now seated at the right hand of the Father at the Throne of Grace?
- Are you absolutely certain that he is going to leave the most holy sanctuary in heaven and return to Earth in bodily form?
- Are you certain?

Certain is an adjective that describes something known for sure, that's established beyond a shadow of doubt.

Certain means something you are confident about; you are absolutely sure of it as a matter of fact.

Let's look at a contrast to certain... it's when you are

uncertain, doubtful, it's not definite, it's not infallible, it's something you cannot "hang your hat on."

Are you absolutely certain that Jesus did everything the Bible says? Or do you think the Bible was only written by men and it's just a set of rules?

Let's see what one of Jesus' disciples had to say about his certainty of the Bible, the infallible Word of God.

"For we did not follow cleverly devised stories when we told you about the coming of our Lord Jesus Christ in power, but we were eyewitnesses of his majesty. He received honor and glory from God the Father when the voice came to him from the Majestic Glory, saying, "This is my Son, whom I love; with him I am well pleased." We ourselves heard this voice that came from heaven when we were with him on the sacred mountain. We also have the prophetic message as something completely reliable, and you will do well to pay attention to it, as to a light shining in a dark place, until the day dawns and the morning star rises in your hearts.

Above all, you must understand that no prophecy of Scripture came about by the prophet's own interpretation of things. For prophecy never had its origin in the human will, but prophets, though human, spoke from God as they were carried along by the Holy Spirit." 2 Peter 1:16-21 (NIV)

Please take time now to study the above scripture, as it is one of the most powerful testimonies in the New Testament.

I believe the Apostle Peter here is trying to get the point over to readers that actually hearing the voice of God and seeing the vision of the transfiguration of Jesus along with the visual visitation of Moses and Elijah should not take the place of the "more sure word of prophecy" alluded to in the above passage. In other words, what we as believers have at our disposal in the scriptures is just as valuable as what Peter, James, and John experienced on the Mount of Transfigurations found in Matthew 17:5 (KJV).

Prayer

Heavenly Father, I thank you that you have given me the certainty that you are my God, that Jesus is my Lord, my elder brother.

I thank you that Jesus is my advocate, my lawyer in the courtroom of life and death.

I thank you that I am certain I am a spirit that I have a soul and a sound mind to make good choices.

I am certain that the Holy Spirit gives me direction by illuminating my mind.

I thank you that as I renew my mind with your Word, I am being transformed into your perfect will for my life.

In Jesus' name, I am certain that you are my Lord!

Amen!

Cistern

Like a reservoir of life within our souls.

"Drink water from your own cistern, running water from your own well. Should your springs overflow in the streets, your stream of water in the public squares?" Proverbs 5:15-16 (NIV)

The word for today is "cistern," which is an underground reservoir for water.

Water, in the natural, represents a life force, and without it, we literally die of thirst. A cistern represents a reserved supply of water or a reserved supply of life, so to speak. Back in the late 1940s, my family lived in a remote area where there was no running water supply. My father dug a round hole about ten feet deep and about three feet in diameter. He sealed the bottom and sides with a thin layer of concrete. He built a wooden folding door to cover the top, and he left an opening in the top just big enough for a tin trough to direct rainwater from the roof of the house down into the ten-foot deep cistern. That cistern was our "natural" life-sustaining source of water. That's the way it is with us as Christians.

The moral of this story is an illustration of how we can sometimes have a misconception of life-giving principles.

I'm reminded of the winter of 2021 while the world experienced a worldwide pandemic called COVID-19 that claimed two-million lives in the previous year. As if that wasn't enough, the greater part of the United States was hit with a winter storm with snow and ice that caused devastating blackouts and left millions of citizens without clean water for drinking, cooking, or cleaning. What a dilemma without the life-giving force of water. Residents had to melt snow and boil tap water before any human use. How nice it would have been to be able to have turned back the hands of time to the thirties and forties when citizens had their own private source of water such as cisterns and wells.

From a spiritual perspective, Proverbs 5:15 tells us to drink water from our own cistern. Here, the Holy Spirit through the Word of God is telling us to be faithful and loyal to our own spouses.

The rest of that verse says, *"And running water from your own well."* Here, we find the cistern is very similar to a well—both contain water which represents life.

However, there is one primary difference between a cistern and a well: in a cistern the water supply comes from the top down, whereas the water in a well flows from an underground stream that comes upward. It's sort of like a spring of running water that is trapped in an underground pool where the stream is contained. Verse 16 asks the question: Should your springs overflow in the streets, your stream of water in the public squares?

It amazes me how God uses a source of water to address infidelity.

Now, let's look at this principle from a contemporary point of view. Three things happen when we drink from our own cistern or well:

First, we know what's in the well.

Secondly, we know how it got there.

Thirdly, we know whether it's good for us or not...quite unlike when we drink from someone else's well.

In contrast, there are a lot of unknowns when drinking from someone else's well:

1. When you drink from another man's well, you don't know who else has been dipping into that well.

2. You don't know if something unhealthy was left in the cistern.

3. If you catch it, you don't if it will be detrimental to your well-being.

4. And if you catch it, you don't know if you can get rid of it before it gets rid of you.

So, we can easily see God's wisdom of drinking water from our own well or cistern and not another man's cistern.

Do you have any idea how many people have lost their lives from catching a foreign substance from another man's cistern? Can you believe there were approximately 2.4 million cases of sexually transmitted diseases in 2018? An excellent example of that was seen in the film entitled *Temptation.*

When we look into the spiritual realm, on the other hand, we see our bodies have a deeply dug and well-prepared life-giving "cistern." The Bible calls it the spirit of man in Proverbs 20:27 (NKJV), which says:

"The spirit of man is the lamp of the Lord, searching all the inner depths of his heart."

In other words, our bodies are the sanctuary for the Spirit of God who lives in the New Testament Christian. It's the place where the life-giving, life-sustaining Holy Spirit of God lives. It is our "cistern" of life . . . not only spiritual life, but mental, emotional, and physical life.

So, we have to learn how to keep our "cistern" full and clean.

I remember one hot Mississippi summer when a great big water moccasin snake crawled off into our life-sustaining cistern. We had to draw all the water out with our bucket and "pulley-chain" and kill the snake. We then had to haul water from a nearby church until it rained again to empty fresh water into our cistern.

The moral of this whole story is to guard your "cistern," which symbolizes your heart, your Spirit, your sanctuary.

Proverbs 4:23 (NKJV) says: *"Keep your heart with all diligence, for out of it spring the issues of life."*

Our issues can be challenges beyond our ability to handle with our own strength. That means we need to make sure our cistern or reserved source of spiritual life is well-maintained. That's done by watching what goes into the cistern—our heart through our eye gate and ear gate. If something ungodly sneaks in, it has to come out one way or the other. Nine times out of ten it's going to come out of the mouth in words, then following with corresponding action.

Prayer

Heavenly Father, help us keep guard over the entrances of our heart.

Father, in the name of Jesus, give us a hunger and thirst for the Living Bread and Water of our spiritual lives.

Forgive us for allowing the little "foxes" that sneak in through unguarded gates of our total beings.

Thank you, Daddy, for hearing and answering our prayers. Amen!

Confess

A process of affirming we believe Jesus is Lord, as well as a process of cleansing of the soul.

"If you confess with your mouth the Lord Jesus and believe in your heart that God raised Him from the dead, you will be saved. For with the heart one believes unto righteousness, and the mouth confession is made unto salvation."Romans 10:9-10 (NKJV)

That scripture represents only half of the context of the word, "confess." When I was a boy living in the rural South, there was a gray wood frame Missionary Baptist Church that had a week-long revival the first week of August.

At the age of twelve, my mother insisted I get on the mourners' bench. It was a pew that was placed down in front of the congregation. There were about ten of us in that age bracket who had to sit on that bench during this week-long revival. That Sunday night, at the beginning, the deacons and mothers of the church sang "Dr. Watts" hymns and read Romans 10, verses 9 and 10.

All of us young mourners were told to get on our knees and repeat that scripture, and confess we were sinners and say, "Lord have mercy on my soul and save me." We were to repeat that, saying it over and over until we were moved involuntarily off that bench by the Lord.

The old folks told us confession was good for the soul, and according to the Bible that's true. The Bible tells us in I John 1:9 (NKJV):

"If we confess our sins, He is faithful and just to forgive our sins and cleanse us from all unrighteousness."

Many of us have thorns in our flesh. So what does it mean to confess? It means to admit, acknowledge, or state that we did something wrong or we're at fault in some way. I believe that type of confession demands that we turn all the way from our sinful way to God's righteous way. That's what the Bible calls repentance.

Even if we confess reluctantly, feeling ashamed or embarrassed about it, confession is still good for the soul. In other words, confession delivers us out of the snares and grasps of Satan.

Sometimes we can be going through a period of depression and cannot understand why. That's the time we need to do like David did in Psalm 51:3 (NKJV) where he said:

"For I acknowledge my transgressions, and my sin is always before me."

We need to act on the knowledge of our sins. Sometimes we just need to step up to the plate and confess, "It's me, I'm the guilty one!" Confession is good for the soul—mind, choices, and emotions.James 5:16 (NLT) says:

"Confess your sins to each other and pray for each

other so that you may be healed. The earnest prayer of a righteous person has great power and produces wonderful results."

Prayer

Father, in the name of Jesus, show us if there's anything going on inside of us that is not pleasing to you—anything that causes us to go contrary to your Word, your will. Bring us under conviction and by your goodness lead us to repentance so that we will confess our faults and be healed. Amen!

Confidence

Believing that we receive what we ask God for when we pray, not when we see it.

"Now, this is the confidence that we have in Him, that if we ask anything according to His will, He hears us." I John 5:14 (NJKV)

Do you ever feel God hears your prayers? "Confidence in God's Word" is what gives that assurance we can rely on. It's an assurance we can have firm trust.

Think about when you got up this morning, did you rely on the chair you sat in to hold you up?

Did you have confidence that you'd be able to walk from your bedroom to the kitchen?

How about the last time you got into your car to go somewhere? Did you believe it was going to start when you turned the ignition switch?

This is an example of the kind of confidence we should have in God's Word!

Just as sure as you trust your legs to work when your mind tells you to get up and go, you should have the same assurance and confidence in God when you petition him for something according to his Word and will.

How can we be so sure that God hears us when we ask him for something?

Good question. Verse 14 tells us, "If we ask anything according to his will, he hears us."

Well, how do we know or have confidence that what we ask for is according to his will? Good question: We will find out in the Word of God. Let's look at two passages of scriptures. Isaiah 43:26 (NKJV) says, "Put Me in remembrance; Let us contend together; State your case, that you may be [a]acquitted." Let's back that up with Isaiah 1:18-20 (NKJV) which says, "Come now, and let us reason together," says the LORD, "Though your sins are like scarlet, They shall be as white as snow; Though they are red like crimson, They shall be as wool. If you are willing and obedient, You shall eat the good of the land; 20 But if you refuse and rebel, You shall be devoured by the sword; For the mouth of the LORD has spoken."

We can't just read the Word of God one time and think we have it. We have to constantly remind ourselves—reason with God about what's in the Word as God said in Joshua 1:8. And if we follow the will, His promises are yes and amen!

2 Corinthians 1:20, (NLT).

We've got to work on changing our reality to believe and stand on the promises of our Father that he's put in the will.

However, our reality is limited and even hampered by the

flesh and physical eyes, but when we keep our spiritual eyes on the Word of God, our confidence becomes a shiftless foundation that is solid as a rock.

Confidence in God's Word is something you can "hang your hat on!"

Prayer

Father God, in the name of Jesus, we thank you for confidence in your holy Word.

We thank you for your promise that you will never leave nor forsake us.

We thank you that you gave us eyes to see, ears to hear, legs to walk, and hands to handle.

We thank you, Father, for confidence in your Word that you have begun a good work in us, and you are faithful to complete it.

We declare that no weapon the devil has formed against us will prosper, and because of your faithfulness, everything we do will prosper. Amen!

Deceiver

If we deceive others, we become subject to being deceived ourselves.

"But evil men and seducers shall wax worse and worse, deceiving, and being deceived." 2 Timothy 3:13 (KJV)

"My people are destroyed for lack of knowledge: because thou hast rejected knowledge, I will also reject thee, that thou shalt be no priest to me: seeing thou hast forgotten the law of thy God, I will also forget thy children." Hosea 4:6 (KJV)

How do these two scriptures work together you may ask? Very well I might add.

If a person is always trying to deceive someone else, they'll have a tendency to forget the truth and fall for another person's lie or deception.

If that happens, when the truth of God's Word is presented, it is unrecognizable and rejected. Then God makes it very clear that he will reject whoever rejects his truth! It's a good thing to stay encouraged but never flattered.

Too often we hear Christians say, "I don't want to mention the name of the evil one too much." I beg your pardon. If we don't recognize the strategies of the opponent, we can lose the game.

The enemy to our success and prosperity in life is a "deceiver." He is a spirit-being, and we cannot see him in the natural.

His personality is charismatic. He's very articulate and conniving with his communication skills. The Bible says, in Ecclesiastes 1:9, "...there is nothing new under the sun." As the deceiver was in Genesis, so is he in Revelation and throughout history.

Not only is he slick, and conniving but he's an awesome entertainer—and you know, we humans loved to be entertained. He knows how to make us laugh, get us high, and do things we will regret when it is all over. How many of you know he doesn't stop when he deceives you, but he takes it to the next level to destroy your fellowship with God and people?

God gave us emotions but He also gave us a mind to think and a will to make choices. How can we make proper choices if we don't have accurate knowledge or information? The evil one knows that. That's why he has to dress up his game so he can deceive us.

Revelation 12:9 (NKJV) describes the biggest deceiver of all times, the "evil one":

"So the great dragon was cast out, that serpent of old, called the Devil and Satan, who deceives the whole world; he was cast to the Earth, and his angels were cast out with him."

He's identified as a:

1) Dragon—big ferocious
2) Serpent—small, inconspicuous, sly, slithery, poisonous, sneaky, quiet, slippery
3) Satan—can operate like a dragon, or like a snake, a prince, an angel of light. As a snake, he can sneak up on you and attack before you know it.
4) Devil—He can function in all four capacities at once or separate. Jesus describes him as a thief, who comes to steal, kill, and destroy.

Satan is just the opposite from Jesus. Satan comes as a sly, sneaky, thief to take away your goods. He'll take your life that Jesus gave. He'll try to steal your family that only God can give.

He disguises his motives and deceives you by making things look one way while all the same time, it's totally another way. It's never the way it looks with the "evil one," but he wants you to think it's you or God.

He deceives people in blaming God for the death of their loved ones, and they stay mad with God for years. When all the same time, it's the killer who did the dirty work. Deception is one of the evil one's most often used tactics.

Jesus says in Matthew 24:24 (KJV):

"For there shall arise false Christs and false prophets, and shall shew great signs and wonders; insomuch that, if it were possible, they shall deceive the very elect."

When Christians think they are giving the devil too much

credit for "evil," guess what... they are deceived.

There're only two sides in this war—good and evil. If it's bad, it's done by Satan or inspired by him. If it is good, no question, it's God or inspired by him.

Again, Jesus says *"the thief comes only to kill, steal, and destroy. But, I have come that they might have life and that more abundantly."(John 10:10, KJV).* "What type of scientist or doctor do we need to explain that theory?

If the "evil one" can throw the rock, hide his hand, and we believe he's innocent, we're in big trouble!

Remember, when we are trying to avoid giving Satan credit, go on give him the credit due him.

1.   He's an accuser and a slanderer.

2.   He's a deceiver.

3.   He's a tempter.

4.   He's a blocker or a hinderer of all that's good from above.

We've got to know our enemy before we can defeat him. We've got to understand his mode of operation and tactics.

Example: The Dallas Cowboys coach would not think of playing an opposing football team without studying their videos and discussing their tactics. So why would we think of going on the battlefield against the enemy of our soul without studying its strategy. The good thing about it is Satan has no new tactics!

Think about what he did in Revelation 12 to get one third of the angels on his side. What makes us think we don't need to know his game plan?

He's an accuser. Revelation 12:10 says:

"...for the accuser of our brethren, who accused them before our God day and night, has been cast down."

Day and Night is all the time. After being cast down, the rascal had the nerve to accuse God of deceiving Adam.

But notice what he did. Satan went to Adam's wife, Eve. The Bible says he was the most subtle, slick, sly, slithery creature in the garden.

I can just see him sliding up to Eve with his gold-colored suit with rust and black stripes, sticking out his tongue talking about that beautiful tree in the middle of the garden.

You don't believe me? Let's look at Genesis 3:1 from NIV:

"Now the serpent was more crafty than any of the wild animals the Lord had made. He said to the woman, 'Did God really say, 'you must not eat from any tree in the garden?'"

You see, right there in that first verse, the evil one casts doubt in the heart of the woman.

Okay, now watch this in verses 2 and 3:

"The woman said to the serpent, 'We may eat fruit from the trees in the garden, but God did say, 'You must not eat fruit from the tree that's in the middle of the garden, and you must not touch it, or you will die.'"

In verse 4, Satan talks back to the woman. He's got her

right where he wants her . . . in doubt. He says, "You will not certainly die." I like what the KJV says, "Ye shall not surely die."

Satan, the smooth talking serpent gave Eve a half truth.

Watch this. "You shall not surely die." Notice he didn't say, "You will not die."

That's exactly how Satan gets so many folks on his side . . . by deceiving them with the half-truth that they don't have but one life to live, like a popular beer commercial says, "You only go around once, grab all the gusto you can."

(The use of this word was inspired by the reading materials of the great Bible teacher, Derek Prince.)

Prayer

Heavenly Father, I thank you for the new birth that gives me access to revelation knowledge, divine wisdom, and spiritual understanding. Father, I thank you for your inspired scriptures in the Holy Bible that shows me the truth to avoid the deceiver in Jesus' name. Amen!

Destiny

Where we're headed in life before it's all over

"And we know that all things work together for good to them that love God, to them who are the called according to his purpose."Romans 8:28 (NKJV)

"The steps of a good man are ordered by the Lord: and he delighteth in his way." Psalm 37:23 (KJV)

Steps are only increments of our destiny. Our destiny in life is predetermined or predestined by THE HOLY God who created us for his divine purpose. God says in our text that "the steps of a good man are ordered by the Lord." But it's up to us as free-willed moral beings to follow the route he has cut out for us. As we look at today's word, "destiny," we'll be interchanging destiny with three other closely-related words...destination, purpose, and vision.

I will never forget May 24, 1963—the day that I caught the Illinois Central train from Batesville, Mississippi to Chicago, for the first time in my life. I arrived at my destination at midnight Sunday. By the following Tuesday, at the tender age of seventeen, I had my first real job...a destiny I'd dreamed about since I was ten years old...a destiny I'd dreamed about while slaving in a plantation cotton field for two dollars a day. Destiny is the fate of every human being with any type of ambition for the American dream. Some succeed, some don't.

Life has many destinies, some natural, some eternal; sort of like that dash found on every headstone in cemeteries.

Life itself is like a journey! Our God-given vision is our destiny. What we do with the vision will determine where we go in life.

In other words, our vision is the GPS to guide us to fulfilling our purpose or destiny. How we use it determines our destiny, or should we say our destination, or where we end up in life.

We can always find out where we stand and where we are headed on God's GPS system—the Word of God and the Holy Spirit—as we read and meditate in the Bible. But our destiny, where we end up, is our choice. It depends on how we use the mind, gifts, and opportunities presented to us in life.

Life is as simple or as complicated as the dash on our grave's headstone. What we do in between sunrise to sunset is up to us. In other words, God created us a free-will moral agent to choose.

A good example of man's freedom of choice is found in Deuteronomy 30:19-20 (NKJV):

"I call heaven and earth as witnesses today against you, that I have set before you life and death, blessing and cursing; therefore, choose life, that both you and your descendants may live. That you may love the Lord your

God, that you may obey His voice, and that you may cling to Him, for He is your life and the length of your days; and that you may dwell in the land which the Lord swore to your fathers, to Abraham, Isaac, and Jacob, to give them."

One of the most significant aspects of life's journey is how we deal with people along the way, which determines how we arrive at our destination.

That word destination has two parts:

1) Desti - is a travel guide.

2) Nation - is a body of people.

So, another aspect of us fulfilling our destiny is, again, determined in great part by how we deal with people; how well we understand people and interact with others on the journey. Simply put, it all boils down to the choices we make that determine our destiny.

Let's look at it another way: If God gave us a freewill, a conscience, and his Word, who's responsible for our destiny? We are!

The first step on our journey called "life" is to give our life to Jesus. The second step is to hunger and thirst for his righteousness.

"I beseech you therefore, brethren, by the mercies of God, that you present your bodies a living sacrifice, holy acceptable to God, which is your reasonable service. And do not be conformed to this world, but be

transformed by the renewing of your mind, that you may prove what is that good and acceptable and perfect will of God."Romans 12:1-2 (NKJV)

Again, our scripture text and post text, tell us:

"And we know that all things work together for good to those who love God, to those who are the called according to His purpose. For whom He foreknew, He also predestined to be conformed to the image of His Son, that He might be the firstborn among many brethren."Romans 8:28-29 (NKJV)

So, we can see from scripture that God had a purpose and a plan for each of us to reach our destination or destiny on the Earth.

Prayer

Father, in the Name of Jesus, we thank you for a hunger to know you better, to fellowship with you as we travel on this journey of life that you have given us.

We believe and receive the truth in your Word that everything we go through is working together for our good because we are called and destined to fulfill your divine purpose for our lives. Amen!

Epistle

Our lifestyle is a spiritual letter that is read by others.

"You are our epistle written in our hearts, known and read by all men; clearly you are an epistle of Christ, ministered by us, written not with ink but by the Spirit of the living God, not on tablets of stone but on tablets of flesh, that is, of the heart." 2 Corinthians 3:2-3 (NKJV)

So, what is an "epistle?" We are!

Let's look at Ezekiel 36:26-27 (KJV):

"A new heart also will I give you, and a new spirit will I put within you: and I will take away the stony heart out of your flesh, and I will give you an heart of flesh. And I will put my spirit within you, and cause you to walk in my statues, and ye shall keep my judgments, and do them."

The born-again new creation of God is a living epistle, a living letter that's been written by God on the tablet of our heart. The English word for epistle is letter—a written letter. What is written is what is read, what is read is what is believed, and what is believed is what is lived. *"For as he thinks in his heart, so is he." (Proverbs 23:7, NKJV). "Out of the abundance of the heart the mouth speaks." (Luke 6:45, KJV).*

This means God has written his desires for us on our hearts so our lives can be letters, read by all people he sends across our paths.

As born-again believers, we are living epistles, letters written by God, our creator, to be read by people he sends us to. Let us never forget that.

I've got news for you…if you thought you were born in the nineteenth or twentieth century, God said he chose you before the foundation of the world. Ephesians 1:4 (NKJV).

You are a living epistle, a letter written by God, signed and sealed with the blood of Jesus and delivered to everybody God has put across your path in life.

Though this may be hard to understand, there is nothing so bad in our lives that God did not allow to be there. But through Christ, we overcome those hurdles—the obstacles, the obstructions, mountains of misunderstanding, fear, worry, doubt, confusion, and sickness.

God says in the letter that he's written on your heart that you are more than a conqueror and that no weapon formed against you shall prosper.

Your very life is a love letter written by God.

Everyone who sees you should be able to read God's message to the world—that he loved it so much that he gave his only begotten Son to save, heal, and deliver his love letter to the world.

Did you know that an epistle or letter is a series or a

combination of marks, signs, and symbols to give information that communicates ideas and messages?

In the same way God chose us before the foundation of the world to be like him, he commands us to write his instructions in our offspring. The scriptures tell us to train up our children in the admonition of the Lord.

We have a tendency to do that by what we say to them and the way we live. They will grow up acting just like us in the same way that we, as born-again believers who have God's spiritual DNA in us, should imitate him.

Let us never forget that we are an epistle, a letter written and sent by God so all the world can read his love message.

Prayer

Father God, we thank you that you are mindful of us; that you breathed yourself into us and gave us your image and made us like you.

We thank you that you made us a little lower than angels and gave us dominion over everything you created in the Earth, even the birds that fly in the air and the fish that swim in water.

We thank you that we are your "special delivery" epistle—letter to the world.

We give you praise, honor, and glory for your majesty and love for us, Amen!

Evil

Anything contrary to God's word.

"And lead us not into temptation, but deliver us from evil..."
Matthew 6:13(KJV)

Deliverance from "evil" comes through the power of the Gospel!

What is evil? In a biblical sense, "evil" is not something; rather, "evil" is someone, a spirit-person whose origin is Satan that cannot be seen or touched to our physical body.

We, as Christians, call ourselves spiritual warriors. In order for us to be successful in spiritual warfare, we've got to come to grips with who the real enemy is.

Ephesians 6:12 (KJV) says, *"We wrestle not against flesh and blood."* In other words, our wrestling opponent is not a human being, but the scripture says our wrestling opponents are invisible, un-physically touchable "spirit-beings." These spirit-beings are identified by God as unseen spirit-beings, called principalities, powers, rulers of darkness, and wickedness in heavenly places.

"Evil" is not the "honk" your spouse is cheating on you with, but "evil" is a spirit-being that's operating behind the scenes. Those spirit-beings are giving commands contrary to the Word and will of God.

Those evil spirit-beings are telling human beings who have not submitted and committed to Jesus, the Word of God, to control other human beings through feelings, sight, taste, and pride.

You see, evil—this invisible spirit-being found its origin in Lucifer, who was later called Satan, the "Dragon," and the devil. Evil has other nicknames called "Slanderer" and "Accuser."

This evil spirit-being hates us because God bought us back with the very life of his Son, Jesus, the Christ. We, as believers in Jesus, are a chosen people who have the privilege of being a royal priesthood.

On a quick historical note, Lucifer, the evil-spirit-being, became "puffed up" with pride because of his great beauty, wisdom, and talent. He was a chief musician in heaven before he decided he wanted equality with God.

Isaiah 14:12-15 and Ezekiel 28:13-17 tell us that this evil-spirit being rebelled against Almighty God. He was slick enough to talk one-third of his fellow angels to take sides with him. So, the Godhead cast him and his deceived-rebellious partners out into outer darkness. That story is revealed explicitly by John, the Revelator, in Revelation 12.

So, let us make no mistake about who the "evil one" is and what his purpose is and how he operates against human-beings who are not submitted to God. The only way we can resist him is by submitting to God. God says when we do that, the evil one will flee from us.

But as long as we walk in pride, we are held captivated-victims of the evil one. In contrast, when we submit to the Word of God, we receive the grace—unmerited favor of God—and we can resist the evil one, and he will flee.

He comes to steal, kill, and ultimately destroy us. One of the first weapons he uses against us is "ignorance," not knowing, and even ignoring the Word of God.

"Lest Satan should take advantage of us; for we are ignorant of his devices." 2 Corinthians 2:11 (NKJV)

When we don't know God's will, Satan takes advantages of us. One of his most powerful invisible weapons is discouragement; if he can get you discouraged and we don't recognize that it is an evil-spirit being, we'll quickly get oppressed, and long-term oppression will lead to depression.

The only way we can come out of that multi-fold wrestling match with that evil-spirit being is to do what God says in Isaiah 61:3—that is, to "Put on the garment of praise for the spirit of heaviness..." or discouragement. The evil spirit of heaviness will, if we allow him, take us to a place called depression. So, we have to fight the good fight of faith, by speaking the word of faith.

Prayer

Father God, in the precious name of Jesus we thank you that you haven't left our souls in the pit of darkness where the prince of darkness can kill, steal, and destroy us.

We thank you that we have the weapons of our warfare and they are not carnal, but they are spiritual and mighty to pulling down the strongholds of the "evil one."

Father, we thank you that we are more than conquerors through Christ Jesus Our Lord, and no weapon that the evil one has formed against us shall prosper. For, we are like that tree that's planted by the rivers of water and out of our bellies shall flow rivers of living water, and we shall bring forth our fruit in due season. In Jesus' name, Amen!

Excitement

It comes from the joy of the Lord that makes us spiritually and emotionally strong.

"For the joy of the Lord is my strength."Nehemiah 8:10 (NJKV)

Before we get into this scripture's key word, strength, I want to expound briefly on one way that I see the Nehemiah 8:10 principle unfolding. One way of looking at joy is excitement. Only God can give us true excitement. Excitement comes not so much from what God does for us but how we perceive what he does for us. When we rejoice in our faith and hope in him, we become strong in his presence. The scripture also tells us that our faith pleases God. In other words, Hebrews 11:6 KJV says, *"Without faith it is impossible to please him."* So, in essence, when we praise him by faith, he gives us his strength. His joy infuses us with excitement and strength. I believe that when we praise God for who is with an outward expression of an inner peace, joy, and happiness, we become strong with an emotion of "excitement." That emotion becomes an outward expression of joy.

In a natural sense, one of the most important locations in a public facility is the "EXIT" sign. It's actually illegal to have a public building without a well-positioned exit sign light. If ever caught in an uncomfortable situation, it's important to be able to get out of it, thus the importance of knowing where the exit options are.

Excitement pretty much works the same way…it's an outward expression of an inward emotion or feeling.

It's like breathing. We take in the breath of life but will die if we don't let it out.

I don't know if you saw the movie, *Waiting to Exhale*, where all these women had taken so much foolishness and abuse from the men in their lives for so long...that they couldn't wait to get together to let it out.

That's the same way it is with life for any of us. There comes a time when we have to let out what's been bottled up on the inside. The best way for that to work is to give God praise, in spite of the circumstances. That praise gives God joy from us, and the joy that God gets gives us strength.

Excited praise is like an internal explosion that breaks out to avoid an internal combustion that will eventually destroy a person.

That's what happened to all the believers on the day of Pentecost. They were all in one place in one accord grieving the absence of their great and powerful leader, the Lord Jesus Christ.

"When the Day of Pentecost had fully come, they were
all with one accord in one place. And suddenly there
came a sound from heaven, as of a rushing mighty wind,

and it filled the whole house where they were sitting. Then there appeared to them divided tongues, as of fire, and one sat upon each of them. They were all filled with the Holy Spirit and began to speak with other tongues as the Spirit gave them utterance." Acts 2:1-4 (NJV)

Additionally, too much heat and light on the inside will cause an explosion if it's not let out in a controlled degree. Excitement is what the prophet Jeremiah sensed when he said, *"The Word is like fire shut up in my bones."* (Jeremiah 20:9, KJV).

When the pressure of wind and fire come upon us, whatever is bottled up on the inside is going to burst out in excitement. So don't be afraid to allow the Holy Spirit to purge you with the excitement of outward praise, and holler, Glory Hallelujah!

One final thought in closing; let us learn to release our bottled-up negative emotions in an outburst of praise to the eternal God, our creator and sustainer of life.

Let us pray.

Prayer

Father God, in the precious name of Jesus, we thank you for your living word is like fire shut up in my bones. You said your Word pierces even to the division of our soul and spirit and of the joints and marrow of the bones. (Hebrew 4:12, KJV abbreviated, paraphrased).

Father, we are excited about all you've done for and through us in Jesus' name. Amen!

Favor

God shows favor to those who visit him often.

"A good man obtains favor from the Lord, but a man of wicked intentions He will condemn." Proverbs 12:2 (NJKV)

As we look at today's word, "favor," let's consider the following questions:

- What is favor?
- Who qualifies for favor?
- Where does favor come from?
- How do we obtain favor?

According to the *Merriam Webster dictionary*, favor is friendly regard shown toward another, especially by a superior. That's more of a man's favor.

But the favor of God is what we need. It's an act of kindness beyond what is deserved. In other words, we don't have to qualify for God's favor!

God's favor is…

- Peaceful, when a man's ways please God.
- Undeserved, but valuable!
- Preferential treatment—that's what God does for believers in Jesus. He gives us the good we don't

deserve and withholds the bad we do deserve.

That brings us to our next question: Who qualifies for this kind of treatment?

The scripture says a good man obtains favor from the Lord. So what do we have to do to be good?

Come to Jesus.... The Bible says "who so ever will" let him come. God is no respecter of persons. Just come as you are, and God will give you undeserved favor and save you!

Too often, we look in the wrong places from the wrong sources for favor. But the only way we can obtain the Lord's favor is to lay aside the weights that so easily beset us and humble ourselves at the foot of the cross.

The favor from God is for us to be a blessing to others.

Prayer

Father, we thank you for your favor, and underserved grace toward us by redeeming and saving us from eternal death and giving us life more abundantly here and now on Earth. We praise and worship you now in the name of Jesus, the Christ. Amen!

Integrity

To be honest with God and people.

"Abstain from every form of evil." I Thessalonians 5:22 (NKJV)

"Integrity" is being upright in behavior with both man and God. Integrity is to be blameless; it means to fear or reverence God.

Integrity helps keep us away from evil and serves as a mental and emotional wall of protection from evil thoughts, words, and actions. Integrity in man serves as a landmark for all those who cross his path. It lets those who see him know God is in the midst.

In Psalm 26:1-4 (NLT), David said:

"Declare me innocent, O Lord, for I have acted with integrity; I have trusted in the Lord without wavering.
Put me on trial, Lord, and cross-examine me. Test my motives and my heart. For I am always aware of your unfailing love, and I have lived according to your truth.
I do not spend time with liars or go along with hypocrites."

This scripture indicates good moral character alone will

not get you into heaven, but encourages us to trust in God without wavering.

I always think about men who were outstanding businessmen, good family men, but didn't believe in Jesus. Integrity alone is not a ticket to heaven, but it can at least get you to the ticket counter.

So, what is integrity? Integrity is manifested in moral uprightness. In Genesis 20, the integrity of a king saved his life. *(Please take time to read this entire chapter.)*

Here the lack of integrity is represented by unselfish service:

"Then Moses was very angry, and said to the Lord, 'Do not respect their offering. I have not taken one donkey from them, nor have I hurt one of them.'" Numbers 16:15 (NJKV)

Integrity is manifested in the keeping of vows:
"Then came the word of the Lord to Jeremiah..." Jeremiah 35:12 (KJV)

Integrity is demonstrated when we reject bribes and we pay our debts as promised.

A few men of the Bible who demonstrated a life of integrity are Job, David, Daniel, and Paul.

David said, "Put me on trial Lord, and cross examine me. Test my motives and my heart! *For I am always aware of your unfailing love." Psalm 26:2 (NLT).*

A person can be honest, upright, and good and still not be born of the Spirit of God. Jesus said a person cannot even understand the kingdom of God until he or she is born from heaven.

In essence, there are a lot of good people who are well-respected with great integrity, yet they are still pleasing to God.

The Apostle Paul says, in 1 Corinthians 13:3 (NKJV):

"And though I bestow all my goods to feed the poor, and though I give my body to be burned, but have not love, it profits me nothing."

So, integrity that pleases God is having the Spirit of God in our heart living blameless lives before God and man.

Prayer

Heavenly Father, I thank you for leading me in your path of right standing with you through my Lord, Jesus Christ. I thank you for prompting the Holy Spirit to bring me under conviction whenever I am tempted to go contrary to your will. In Jesus' name I pray. Amen!

Hero

Friendship with Jesus makes us victorious over the villain.

"This great dragon—the ancient serpent called the devil, or Satan, the one deceiving the whole world—was thrown down to the earth with all his angels. Then I heard a loud voice shouting across the heavens, It has come at last- salvation and power and the Kingdom of our God, and the authority of his Christ For the accuser of our brothers and sisters has been thrown down to earth the one who accuses them before our God day and night.[11] And they have defeated him by the blood of the Lamb and by their testimony. And they did not love their lives so much that they were afraid to die. Revelation 12:9-11(NLT)

Our short lesson today is an appetizer to make us hungry for more manna from heaven—a look at the "hero" and the villain.

Ever since I was a little boy, I have always been fascinated by movies. Even when I was in the first grade my teacher chose me to be in a school play called "Goldilocks and the Three Bears."

As I grew older, I got hooked on the hero-villain roles in movies. I always loved the way screenplay writers escalated the dramatic scenes between the good guy and the bad guy.

Can you imagine a drama where there is no opposition

between the hero and the villain?

A good screenplay writer never makes the role of the hero as important as the villain. Unless the story has a strong villain, no one is going to care about the potential hero.

Superman is a great example. No one would really care about Superman's extraordinary powers or his love for Lois Lane if he were not forced to do battle with the diabolical Lex Luther.

The concept of "hero vs the villain" is not for the silver screen but also for the controversy of good vs. evil on planet Earth.

As we study the Bible, we learn that Lucifer, or Satan, challenged our great hero, Jesus the Christ, from the corridors of heaven to the Garden of Eden. Satan's plan was to separate Adam and Eve from their creator, God, by tempting them to disobey his commandment and to eat from the tree of knowledge of good and evil.

My wife and I often watch the series of *Columbo* movies. In every one of the episodes, right up front, the bad guy who appears to be a good guy does all his dirty work. But about one-fourth of the way into the movie, the Los Angeles Police sends Lieutenant Columbo, the hero, in to defeat the bad guy. The bad guy thinks he's got the upper hand on Columbo, but he's no match.

It's the same way with Satan, the villain on the world's stage. He thought he'd beat God by conquering Adam and Eve.

Oh, but God! God decided to put on his superhero Earth

suit and clothe himself in human flesh in the name of Jesus and come down to Earth and show Lucifer a thing or two. Old slew foot thought he was something—Isaiah 14 says he thought to set up his throne above the throne of God. He thought he was the greatest musician and the most beautiful creature God made and decided he was going to take over heaven and Earth! So, God had to send in reinforcement to kick Satan out of heaven.

Now, here he is on the Earth. . . a place without any form, empty and full of darkness. With a little bit of deception over Adam and Eve, he thought he had beat God. But how many of you know he deceived himself? Since the first Adam couldn't handle it, God sent in reinforcement—the last Adam—the one and only Jesus, The Christ, the Lion from the Tribe of Judah, the Chief Cornerstone of the Church, God's body.

Ah! Satan thought he'd beat God when he took over the great world empires of Babylon, Medo-Persia, Greece, and then the Roman Empire.

The book of Daniel Chapter 2, verse 44 (NKJV) describes how God put Satan in his place. It says in the last days, "God will set up a kingdom which shall never be destroyed; and the kingdom of God shall not be left to other people; it shall break into pieces and put an end to all these other kingdoms and the kingdom of God, a royal priesthood, a holy nation, shall stand forever."

Prayer

Heavenly Father, I am so grateful for your deliverance plan through your hero of heaven and earth. You have given us the measure of faith so that we can receive your redemption plan that gives us, not only eternal life but life to its fullest measure only through our Lord and Savior Jesus Christ. Amen!

Imitator

A consistent imitation of Jesus guarantees victory over Satan.

"Therefore become imitators of God, copy Him and follow His example as well-beloved children imitate their Father."
Ephesians 5:1 (AMP)

How many of you have ever seen or heard of the *Imitation to Life?*

That word "imitator" reminds me of several things I've observed over the years, but one thing that stands out above them all is a talent show we had when I was in middle school. Here we were in a segregated, all-colored school in the heart of the rural South in the Mississippi Delta. During this time, there was a very popular singer named Elvis Presley. One of the boys in my class decided to imitate Elvis by performing a song entitled "All Shook Up." He came out on the stage with a straw broom in his hands imitating Elvis, and all the girls went absolutely berserk.

That was not strange for us to imitate those who were far removed from our culture in every sense of the word. The other folks just had it better than us. They had better schools, better homes, better cars, and as we blacks used to say. . . better hair. No wonder, an unlearned, un-everything people would want to be like those with everything desirable. Then, there was the movie called *Imitation of Life*.

On the other hand, how many of us really want to be like Jesus? In Ephesians 5:1(NJKV), the Apostle Paul says, *"Therefore be imitators of God, dear children."*

What do you think the world would look like if we Christians would really imitate Jesus?

What Jesus Did

Let's take a quick look at what Jesus did that we, the church, could be doing to make this world a better place. Just think about it!

In the 1980s, there was a popular acronym called WWJD-What Would Jesus Do?

Based on the Gospel—the Power of God

Q: What would Jesus do when he saw invisible tormentors harassing, manipulating, and controlling the lives of people?

A: He cast out the evil spirits.

Q: What would Jesus do when he saw people lame and cripple?

A: He reached out and touched them, and they were healed.

So, if we were to become imitators of Jesus, what would we do? Would we do like my schoolmate who took a broom and sang and gyrated his body to imitate Elvis, or would we take up our cross as we followed Jesus around the bus stations and skid rows of our city streets?

Jesus said in John 14:12 (NKJV):

"...he who believes in Me, the works that I do, he will do also; and greater works than these he will do, because I go to My Father."

John 7:38 (KJV) says:

"He that believeth on me, as the scripture hath said, out of his belly shall flow rivers of living water."

If we continue in his Word, we shall know the truth, and the truth shall make us free. Free from what? Free from fear of the tormentors, free from poverty, free from rejection, free from promiscuous behavior, free, free, free indeed!

If only we would become imitators of Jesus! Since the whole world is a stage, how many of us Christians are playing our part and truly imitating Jesus?

Prayer

Father, in the name of Jesus our Lord, please give us a hunger and thirst for the living bread and water from heaven that we may imitate the life of our elder brother, Jesus!

Father, I ask you to give us a sincere desire to imitate Jesus and go into all the world and preach the Gospel, cast out evil spirits, and lay hands on the sick and see them recover.

Father, help us to believe Jesus when he said in John 14:12, "the works that I do, you will do also, and greater works than these you will do because I go to my Father." Thank you, Jesus, for praying that we will take up our cross and imitate you. Amen!

Mediator

The Holy Spirit is the mediator who resides within the born-again believer and gives access to the presence of God, the Father.

"For there is one God, and one mediator between God and men, the man Christ Jesus;" I Timothy 2:5 (KJV)

The watchword for today is "mediator." The NIV translation of our verse from I Timothy 2:5 says between *"God and mankind,"* while The New Living Translation uses the word "humanity." In other words, there's one God, and one mediator between God and people. The one mediator is the man, Christ Jesus.

I Timothy 2:6 (KJV) says:

"Who gave himself a ransom for all, to be testified in due time."

In addition to the word, mediator, there are two more words included in those two verses that we need to define to help us put our keyword, mediator, into context—ransom and testified.

A mediator is someone who stands in between two parties who are in conflict with others. Like a defense attorney in criminal court, a mediator stands between the law and grace. The mediator's job is to bring the opposing parties into harmony and agreement.

In the first covenant, Moses was the mediator between God and his people, Israel. That didn't really work, though. While God was giving Moses guidelines for the peoples' behavior, they were building an idol to worship.

So, God prepared himself an Earth suit and came down into the body of his holy Word and became flesh as Jesus. This allowed him to, not only be with mankind, but to get into the heart of man, so he could lead and guide us into the full truth of his omnipotence, omniscience, and omnipresence. All of this takes us back to our word for today, mediator.

Testified, as used in verse 6 of I Timothy 2 means "to witness," or "to give evidence."

The Holy Spirit inspired the Apostle Paul to instruct Timothy to be a witness and give evidence that Jesus, the Christ, is a ransom to God, the Father, for us who had a death sentence hanging over our heads because of sin.

As our mediator, Jesus is the only one who can ultimately stand before God and mankind. Buddha can't do it, because he's still dead. Muhammad can't do it because he's still in his tomb. Confucius can't mediate for us before God.

God required a living sacrifice to be a ransom for our death sentence. Jesus is the only one who came down from God, who lived without sin, and who was qualified to die for the sins of mankind.

But here's the good news of the Gospel—the power of God unto salvation—deliverance for us from the sentence of death…on the third day God the Father, raised God the Son from the dead.

After forty days of final planning and preparation with his disciples on Earth, Jesus was taken back up to heaven where he now lives forever in the presence of God the Father as the only one qualified to be the official mediator. Let us honor Jesus as the only one qualified to erase our sins.

Moses couldn't do it! Abraham couldn't do it! Elijah couldn't do it!

Only one man who ever walked this Earth among men is able to stand in the gap on our behalf before God and be assured, beyond a shadow of doubt, that we are declared not guilty for the penalty of our sins; and that is Jesus, the Christ.

We as believers are admonished to go into all the world and tell the story of how we overcome the trials and tribulations of this life. It's by and through the sinless blood of an unblemished Lamb of God, Jesus the Christ.

Prayer

Father, thank you for your plan of deliverance. Thank you for giving Jesus the ministry of mediation and reconciliation to bring restoration to your people. In Jesus' name, Amen!

Path

Those who've been justified by faith in Jesus are led on the path into the presence of God.

"He restores my soul; He leads me in the paths of righteousness For His name's sake."Psalm 23:3 (NKJV)

Today's watchword is "path" taken from the Twenty-third Psalm, which most of us know by memory.

As we delve into today's study, first of all, let's consider what a path is.

In the natural realm, a path is a way that is beaten, formed, or trodden by the feet of people or animals. It's also used as a shortcut to somewhere. When I was a little boy we'd cut across the field.

In other words, a path is a narrow walkway, a route or a course that's used to direct us to someplace. A path can be a track along which something moves like a train, it goes and comes the same way every time it moves! And finally, a path can be dangerous like the path of a hurricane, which sows destruction.

Now, that we've heard again what a path is for, let me ask you a question: What path are you on? What is the path of your life at this stage?

The writer of Psalm 23 was trained as a little boy to be a

shepherd. And a good shepherd was absolutely necessary to lead a very valuable animal into and through a good, prosperous path where there was good, green grazing with plenty of fresh, still water along the way.

Guess what? If the sheep did not follow the voice of the good shepherd, he would drift off the path somewhere and get lost from the flock and the shepherd.

But how many know that the Good Shepherd, our Father in heaven, would leave the ninety-nine and go find the one lost sheep?

Let's look at some of the paths that sheep can drift off on:

1) We as sheep can choose the path of the wicked. But Job 24:13 says the way or the path of the wicked is dark; they rebel against the Light; the Light blinds them because their evil lifestyle is revealed.

Solomon says in Proverbs 1:15, the path of the wicked is crooked, and *Isaiah 59:8* says, it leads to death.

2) Then we have the path of the believer. It's hindered by the wicked but it's enriched by the Lord; it's upheld by the Lord and directed by God and given Light by Christ Jesus.

3) The third type of path we want to discuss is the path of righteousness.

Isaiah 53:6 (KJV) says:

"All we like sheep have gone astray; we have turned everyone to his own way; and the Lord hath laid on

Him (Jesus) the iniquity of us all."

Jesus is the Good Shepherd, completely the opposite of the adversary, the evil one called Satan, whose whole purpose is to lead us astray. But God...he gave the Good Shepherd who laid down his life for God's sheep!

He didn't come to the altar like other shepherds and place a sacrifice. The Good Shepherd got up on the altar and became the sacrifice.

How many of us truly know the Good Shepherd today?

How many of us can submit our entire lives like the sheep in pasture into the care of the good Shepherd?

The Bible says in Psalm 23 that *"the Lord is my Shepherd."* And because I've allowed him to be my shepherd, I shall not want, I shall not lack any good thing. Because he makes me to lie down and rest in green pastures, he provides for all my needs according to his riches in glory. He leads me beside still, calm, peaceful water and restores my soul and my mind from worry, fear, and doubt.

I trust him with all my heart and refuse to wander off into the pathway of darkness; off into the cosmic forces of the universe, looking for a sign in the stars.

The Good Shepherd leads me in the paths of righteousness, and in my path is life more abundantly and forever.

Prayer

Father, thank you for leading me down the path of righteousness. Amen!

Planting

Seeds are given by God to plant, not eat. Instead, he gives bread to eat.

"To appoint unto them that mourn in Zion, to give unto them beauty for ashes, the oil of joy for mourning, the garment of praise for the spirit of heaviness; that they might be called trees of righteousness; the planting of the Lord, that He might be glorified." Isaiah 61:3 (KJV)

"And he shall be like a tree planted by the rivers of water, that bringeth forth his fruit in his season." Psalm 1:3 KJV

The word for today is "planting." We took it from these two passages of scripture from the Old Testament, which inspire me tremendously!

When we are the planting of the Lord, there are several great and exciting things that happen to and for us. Being planted means to be stabilized in and by the one we can trust.

Before we go any further, let's pose four good news questions that we can look to for the answers in these words of wisdom today.

- First, where are planted?
- Secondly, why are we planted?
- Thirdly, for what purpose were we planted?

- Fourthly, who planted us?

Have you ever been on a road trip that took you through a rural farm area? You look out across the fields and see rich, green, flourishing plants with tall, sophisticated irrigation systems? However, you travel only eight or ten miles down the highway and see a field with brown, dried-up scrawny plants. Why do you think it was such a drastic difference between the fields located in the same environmental conditions? You think it may have been the planter, the conditions of soil, or a combination of both?

Matthew 15:13 NJKV gives us some insight:

"...Every plant which my heavenly Father has not planted will be uprooted."

Here's the answer. The reason the one field flourished and the other one didn't lie in the planter. Now, the next question to ponder is who did the planting?

Let's look at the difference between the two planters. One planter counted the cost before beginning the process, and the other one didn't.

Prayer

Father, may I always be willing and obedient to "count the cost" and follow you. Amen!

Purge

Admitting you're wrong when guilty of sin gives God permission to purge or squeeze out all unrighteousness.

"I will purge the rebels from among you, and those who transgress against Me; I will bring them out of the country where they dwell, but they shall not enter the land of Israel. Then you will know that I am the Lord." Ezekiel 20:38 (NKJV)

The word for today is "purge." What does it mean? Purge means to cleanse thoroughly, completely through, leaving no residue of contamination.

An example of the purging process in the natural is the twenty seconds of "hand-washing" to get rid of any microscopic germs or viruses that may be passed to our mouth, nose, and eyes that might contaminate us with COVID-19.

In other words, we want to crucify or kill anything foreign that could infiltrate our immune system. Once a virus gets into our cellular system, it can take over the entire operational system of the body.

That's why God said in the text that he was going to purge the rebels, those who were contrary to his operation from among his people, Israel.

You see, Israel, in the first covenant, did not have a

spiritual immune system that was able to fight off sin. "A little leaven would leaven the whole lump," meaning that the least bit of sin would contaminate the whole tribe. Instead, God set up a quarantine for his people by removing or purging sinners from them.

In the new covenant that God has made with believers in Christ Jesus, he has given us his power within to help purge ourselves from foreign spirits that can contaminate our souls, our minds, our choices, and emotions.

Through Christ Jesus, God regenerates our spiritual immune system through repentance, forgiveness, consecration, and sanctification.

In Psalm 51, the Psalmist David, a man after God's own heart, recognized and admitted he sinned against God and man. He asked God to wash him thoroughly from his iniquity and cleanse him from his sin. Then he asked God in Psalms 51:7 to purge him with "hyssop" so that he would be clean.

In the Old Testament God purged his people, but in the New Testament, how are we to be purged? We all should be purged from the traditions of men so we can be free to live by the Word of God. This purging process is only available through accepting Christ Jesus as Savior. If you have not yet done so, I encourage you to contact me or someone you trust as a Godly mentor.

Prayer

Father, thank you for the cleansing blood of Jesus Christ, that we might be saved. In Jesus' name we pray. Amen!

Ransom

God gave up his only begotten Son as a ransom for the guilty.

"For there is one God and one Mediator between God and men, the Man Christ Jesus, who gave Himself a ransom for all, to be testified in due time." I Timothy 2:5-6 (NKJV)

"Ransom" is a payment demanded for the release of a hostage. Although we may not have realized it, we were hostages bound in iniquity and sin.

Satan, the father of lies, the deceiver of all mankind, the one who instigates all evil, inflicts all kinds of deadly sickness and diseases upon God's heritage. Then God turned around and gave up his only begotten Son to be the ransom to redeem us back from the devil.

The good news for believers is we've been delivered from the power of the world system into the kingdom of God. We were held as captives, but God sent his Son Jesus as our ransom to get us back.

When I think of a ransom, the first thing that comes to my mind is the movie Mel Gibson starred in. He had amassed a great deal of wealth. So, the criminals kidnapped his son for a two-million-dollar ransom.

Just think about how much God loved us while we were yet sinners in our mess, that he gave his only begotten Son to be a ransom for us.

Consider how many of God's precious souls are being held hostage by Satan and his entourage for no other reason than to kill, steal, and destroy.

But God in Christ Jesus says, "I've come that they may have life, and may have it more abundantly." John 10:10b (KJV).

Throughout today when we are hit by forces beyond our control, just remember that Jesus paid the ransom, and we are free!

Prayer

Father, we thank you that you desire no one be lost but that everybody would come to repentance and be delivered.

Your Word says the harvest is plenty, but the laborers are few. We ask you to send laborers across the path of those who are in darkness and draw them to the light of your truth.

We believe that we receive it now as we pray, so we give you thanks for many hostages held by Satan to be set free in Jesus' name. Amen!

Reprieve

Another chance to get it right, according to God's will.

"Remember, the sins of some people are obvious, leading them to certain judgment. But there are others whose sins will not be revealed until later." I Timothy 5:24 (NLT)

"Reprieve" is an opportunity to get it right—an escape, either permanently or temporarily from an expected punishment or consequences.

A good example of reprieve is when you've messed up on the job and you should have been fired for it but your boss decided to give you another chance. That's a reprieve.

Think about it... How many times have we sinned before God and he gave us a reprieve? Even those times when we messed up and didn't even realize it was sin.

That scripture text alone sobers me up. That's the grace of God giving a reprieve—an opportunity to escape the next temptation to do it again.

Even when we are about to sin with our mouth sometimes, an interruption will block it.

That's an escape where a reprieve is still working on our behalf trying to help us get it right.

That's the time to thank God and ask him to regulate our minds, because as a man thinks, so is he and out of fullness of the heart the mouth speaks.

James 3:8 (NIV) says:

"but no human being can tame the tongue. It is a restless evil, full of deadly poison."

Too many times we sin with our tongue even to the point of committing spiritual murder as in Proverbs 18:21 (NIV), which says:

"The tongue has the power of life and death, and those who love it will eat its fruit."

So, let us thank God for giving us a reprieve by not allowing the consequences of our sins to catch up with us before we can repent.

God is such a gracious and merciful God. He gave us his Word in I Corinthians 10:13. He promises us that he will not allow any temptation to overtake us so we will not be able to bare it but will always make a way of escape. Thank God for Jesus!

We'll close this devotional with Galatians 6:7 from the King James Amplified which says:

"Do not be deceived, God is not mocked, He will not allow Himself to be ridiculed, nor treated with contempt nor allow His precepts to be scornfully set aside… for whatever a man sows this and this only is what he will reap." Galatians 6:7 Amplified Bible (AMP)

God has given us a stay of execution, a reprieve, by giving us a chance to get it right. That's why he says:

"There hath no temptation taken you but such as is common to man: but God is faithful, who will not suffer you to be tempted above that ye are able; but will with the temptation also make a way to escape, that ye may be able to bear it." 1 Corinthians 10:13 (KJV)

Prayer

Father, in the name of Jesus thank you for your reprieves and open the eyes of understanding to always reveal your way of escape from the temptation to sin against you. In Jesus' name, Amen!

Revival

God uses revival to restore our soul—mind, will, and emotions.

"...I dwell in the high and holy place, with him also that is of a contrite and humble spirit, To revive the spirit of the humble, and to revive the heart of the contrite ones." Isaiah 57:15b (NKJV)

- What is "revival" and who needs reviving?
- What is it good for?
- When is it needed?
- Why is it needed?
- How do we recognize the need?
- How do we know when it comes?
- How do we get revived?

Each of the aforementioned questions are addressed in the Book of Psalms in the Bible.

Meanwhile, there is a restaurant in Minneapolis, Minnesota called "Revival." It specializes in dry-rubbed wings, fried green tomatoes, and fresh farm greens.

Can you just imagine how refreshing it would be to sit down with family and friends for a good "revival meal"? What a feast for the body!

But has your soul ever been hungry for bread from

heaven?

The Psalmist David tells us how he gets his hungry soul replenished.

In Psalm 119:25-26 (NKJV), David said, *"My soul clings to the dust; Revive me according to Your Word. I have declared my ways and you have answered me..."*

When we declare our ways, our mishaps, weights, and sins which so easily beset us, we are drawing near to God, and he'll revive us.

When we confess our faults, God is faithful to forgive us and revive our souls. One song I especially enjoy listening to, mentions a hole in the soul and how God can deliver by filling the hole with his love, grace, and mercy.

Did you know that when we need "revival," the only thing that satisfies is the truth and faithfulness found only in the Word of God. Food, money, fancy houses, cars, wine, women, or song cannot revive us.

When we need revival of our soul—our mind, choices, and feelings—we need to take a lesson from David when he was about to be stoned to death by his own men. He sat down and took inventory of the goodness of God in Psalm 103.

We need to bless the Lord with everything in us and reminisce about God's benefits package:

- He forgave all our iniquities.
- He heals all our diseases.
- He redeems our lives from destruction.

-        He crowns us with living kindness and tender mercies.

Then, he'll send us "Revival" Restaurant and satisfy our mouths with good things so our youth is renewed like the eagles; we can then run and not be weary. We can walk and not faint.

Prayer

Father God, in the precious name of Jesus, we thank you for making this gracious benefits package available to all believers who walk not after the flesh but delight in your Holy Spirit. Amen!

Soul

An Englishman once said, "Above all else, know thyself."

"For what is a man profited, if he shall gain the whole world, and lose his own soul?"Matthew 16:26 (KJV)

This scripture asks one of the most profound questions ever, as the "soul" is the most vital asset of human existence. Do you know what the soul really is?

"Let him know that he who turns a sinner from the error of his way will save a soul from death and cover a multitude of sins." James 5:20 (NKJV)

How is that….one sinner who becomes born again from spiritual death to spiritual life will be a seed that God plants into humanity; and many who are dead in their trespasses and sins will be engrafted into the kingdom of God.

"The soul who sins shall die." Ezekiel 18:4(NKJV)

James 1:21 (NKJV) says:

"Therefore, lay aside all filthiness and overflow of wickedness, and receive with meekness, the implanted word, which is able to save your souls."

Notice the verse says lay aside—that's an act of our will or an exercise of our power of choice. To lay aside means to move it out of the way with special care.

The scripture tells us to let every word be established in the mouth of two or three witnesses.

With that principle, let's take a look at Hebrews 12:1(NKJV):

"... lay aside every weight, and the sin which so easily ensnares us, and let us run with endurance the race that is set before us."

Another translation says, "so easily entangles us " In other words, things that entrap us. With those admonishments, there is a set of principles that will help us keep a bridle on our soul.

First of all, let's understand what the components of the soul are.

We know that we, as human beings, were created in the image of God. This is recorded in Genesis 1:26 (NJKV) where God said, *"Let Us make man in Our image, according to Our likeness."*

Now, that takes us to the image of God. When we talk image, the first thing that comes to mind is the way something looks or appears to the eyes.

John 1:18 (NKJV) says, *"No one has seen God at any time."* The B part of that verse says, *"The only begotten Son, who is in the bosom of the Father, He has declared Him."*

Colossians 2:9 (NKJV) says, *"For in Him dwells all the fullness of the Godhead bodily."*

Hebrews 1:3(NKJV) says, Jesus is *"the express image of His person."*

That takes us back to the creation concept; again, God said in Genesis 1:26 (NKJV), *"Let us make man in Our image, according to Our likeness."* This refers to the Father, Son, and Holy Spirit. Remember, verse 27 says, *"So God created man in His own image."* The word "our," refers to God, the Father, God the Son, and the Holy Ghost. If the Triune God made man in his Triune likeness, mankind must have a Triune or three-fold nature.

Let's confirm that statement in I Thessalonians 5:23B (KJV) which says, *"I pray God your whole spirit, soul and body be preserved blameless unto the coming of our Lord Jesus Christ."*

So mankind lives in an earthly temple, called a body. He has a soul; but he is a spirit in the image and likeness of the Godhead—God the Father, God the Son-Jesus, and God the Holy Spirit.

If we really pay attention to the "Word of God" the Bible answers itself. So, we let all principles become established and confirmed in the mouths of two or three witnesses.

Notice what Jesus says in Mark 8:36 (KJV). *"For what shall it profit a man, if he shall gain the whole world, and lose his own soul."*

Now, again, what is the soul? We know it is part of the non-material, non-physical intangible part of humans—the soul is not the body. We know the soul is not the earthly house that we can see, touch, or taste, right? If we can't touch, taste, nor see the soul it must be spiritual.

God says the soul needs to be saved. He says in James 1:21 that the engrafted word is able to save your souls.

What is in the Word that makes it unique enough to save our souls?

What is so important about the soul that it needs to be and can be saved, healed, and delivered? Lots of folks believe that when you're dead, you're done.

Thankfully, this is simply not the case. The soul is part of God's image and likeness. Our soul consists of three parts: our mind, our will or choices, and our feelings or emotions.

One of the most devastating things that can happen to us is somebody cuts us down and hurts our feelings. The psychiatrist business is booming because of damaged emotions.

How many of us know that God's Word has a balm to heal damaged emotions and sin-sick souls?

That's why God tell us to become transformed by the renewing of our minds!

Let's look in the mirror again and see what image God sees in us. Again, James says the Word of God is the mirror that reflects the perfect law of freedom for us.

But before we look back in the mirror, let's look briefly at two thirds of the soul, which is made up of mind and will or power of choices.

We will not make good choices if we don't have the correct mind, information, or knowledge.

Hosea 4:6 (KJV) says:

"My people are destroyed for lack of knowledge..."

Here he's talking about how God's people, born-again believers, are destroyed for lack of knowledge.

That's why God, our Father, through his Son, Jesus Christ, by the teaching, the leading and comfort of the Holy Spirit will guide us into all truth.

The last scripture for this lesson is found in Hebrews 4:12 (NKJV), which says:

"For the word of God is living and powerful, and sharper than any two-edged sword, piercing even to the division of soul and spirit, and of joints and marrow, and is a discerner of the thoughts and intents of the heart."

In other words, the skillful use of the Word of God operates on our soul like a scalpel in the hand of a skillful surgeon who operated on our body.

Now, that we know who we are and who we belong to, we can keep our soul from being lost. Let's consider the mental, emotional, and power tools we can use to be successful in getting our souls saved, healed, and set free for this life and eternity.

I call them the principles of soul success. Each principle starts with a "D." The first is desire. David said, *"Delight yourself also in the Lord, And He shall give you the desires of your heart." Psalm 37:4 (NKJV).*

The second D stands for discipline. We have to discipline our flesh—to press our way into the presence of God.

"Enter into his gates with thanksgiving, And into his courts with praise. Be thankful to him, and bless his name." Psalm 100:4 (NKJV)

The third D stands for determination—to refuse to let anything or anybody, not even the devil, stop you from reaching your destination.

And the last D stands for delight. It wraps all the way back around to the top. Delight thyself also in the Lord and he will give you the desires of your heart.

In other words, when we put in the time and effort, God will put his desires in our heart. So, now we know what the soul is and how it functions, we don't have to lose it.

"What does it Profit a man to gain the whole world and lose his soul, But what will a man give in exchange for soul?" Matthew 16:26 (NKJV)

Prayer

Father, in the name of Jesus, I pray that you give us an insatiable desire to understand ourselves as you do. Give us a hunger for your Word so that we may be able to rightly understand what you say about us that we can know beyond a shadow of doubt who we really are deep down inside. Father, we believe that we receive, even now as we pray that you have already answered our request. Thank you and praise your Holy name, Jesus! Amen!

Sower

One who scatters that which is good.

Then He spoke many things to them in parables, saying: "Behold, a sower went out to sow. Matthew 13:3 NKJV)

Life is like a field; from the seeds we sow is the harvest we reap.

The word for today is "sower," the one who scatters. It comes out of a story Jesus told a group of his disciples and bystanders about how the kingdom of heaven works.

Jesus shared a lot of principles of how the kingdom of heaven operates. But this one parable in Matthew 13:1-15 makes a lot of sense to me. I guess it's because I grew up in an agriculture society where we survived by understanding the laws of reproduction.

³ Then He spoke many things to them in parables, saying: "Behold, a sower went out to sow. ⁴ And as he sowed, some seed fell by the wayside; and the birds came and devoured them. ⁵ Some fell on stony places, where they did not have much earth; and they immediately sprang up because they had no depth of

earth. ⁶ But when the sun was up they were scorched,
and because they had no root they withered away.⁷ And
some fell among thorns, and the thorns sprang up and
choked them. ⁸ But others fell on good ground and
yielded a crop: some a hundredfold, some sixty, some
thirty. ⁹ He who has ears to hear, let him hear!"
Matthew 13:3-9 (NKJV)

In this passage Jesus tells the story about how this dirt farmer used the most valuable assets he had—seeds.

Please take time to read and reflect on this passage so you can get a clear picture of this word, sower. Now, that you've read the story you can see my points in this lesson.

If you are a farmer with land and no seed, you're in trouble! But if you've got seed and land, all you need is the wisdom of when and how to plant!

Jesus goes on to tell the story of how the farmer used his sack of seed to get a harvest. According to the story there was nothing wrong with the seed the farmer had. But the problem was found with how he used the seeds and where he planted.

Let's go back and see what the farmer did wrong with his precious commodity, the seeds.

Read verses 3-9 and ask yourself the following questions:

• 	Why didn't all the seed bring forth a good harvest?

• 	Was anything wrong with the seed?

• 	Was it the wrong season?

- What went wrong that all the seed did not yield its full potential?

All the seed was good. There was nothing wrong with the sower's hands.

There was nothing wrong with the sower's feet or eyes. So why didn't all the seed come up and multiply into thirty, sixty, and one-hundred times?

Everything was good! There was good soil! There was good seed! It was the right season for planting! The problem must have been with the lack of wisdom of the sower!

Here's a valuable lesson for us as believers in Christ Jesus. If the sower had selected only the good soil to plant the good seed, he would have gotten good results; thirty, sixty, and one hundred-fold from all the seeds he planted.

Let this parable serve as a valuable lesson for us. We need to be mindful of how we use the gifts, talents, and resources God has given to us. He wants us to be good stewards of his resources. So, let us not be careless distributors of our valuables. Let us make sure we seek God first, and he will make sure all our good seeds will bring forth a one hundred-fold.

Remember the following truths about being a good steward of the sowing and reaping process:

- We always reap what we sow.
- We reap more than we sow.
- We reap later than we sow.

Prayer

Father in the name of Jesus, help us not cast our pearl under the feet of swine. Help us to learn to strategically plant our words in good soil that will take root and bear the fruit of the Spirit. Help us not be lackadaisical in the call on our lives. For we know that words fitly spoken are like apples of gold in a pitcher of silver. In Jesus' name, Amen!

Spue

Luke-warmness is detestable to God. To avoid the spue, turn up the heat.

"So then, because you are lukewarm and neither cold nor hot, I will spue you out of my mouth" Revelation 3:16 (KJV)

Today's word, "spue," means to spit or vomit, to quickly get rid of. Do you think God is serious about spitting us out or getting rid of us?

Think about it—whenever we taste something that's nasty, as youngsters say, we quickly spit it out. We spue it out all over the place. We'll run to a trash can or anywhere as long as we get it out of our mouth.

When we take inventory of our personal and spiritual lives, what is it that's lukewarm? What is it that God or your conscience has been nagging you about?

As I studied the word, "lukewarm," I remembered how much I hate lukewarm coffee. I want it hot or not at all, definitely not lukewarm!

A lukewarm person shows little zeal or enthusiasm. So many times, I don't demonstrate the zeal in winning souls as I should. I know that disappoints God.

Jesus used the word, "lukewarm," when admonishing us

as Christians. The implied meaning of lukewarm in our text is "repulsive," to the point of Jesus spitting us out.

Proverbs 23:7 (KJV) says, *"As a man thinks in his heart, so is he."*

We, as Christians, are not lukewarm because we want to be, but because the "evil one" has gotten an upper hand on our thinking. He has found a flaw in our character, and his subtle strategies make us give in to it. That's exactly where the devil wants us, too.

On the other hand, we, as believers in Christ Jesus, are not helpless victims in situations that the devil perpetrates. One way we can defeat the enemy is to first recognize that Jesus has baptized us with the Holy Ghost and fire and has given us authority over all the power of the enemy according to Luke 10:19.

When we sense the water of the Word of God becoming lukewarm, we've got to immediately put some wood on the fire and heat up the water. Because if we don't stir up the Holy Ghost fire and put some more wood on it, the fire will go out, and we, as believers, stand a chance of becoming lukewarm or even cold. We sure don't want that to happen, do we?

Lukewarm Christians have three outstanding attributes:

1) **Vulnerability**—When we are lukewarm, we are an easy target for the evil one.

2) **Frustration**—When we get frustrated, the spirit of pride creeps in. We have a tendency to lose self-

control. "Who does she think I am? Talking to me like that!" We start talking loudly and cutting the person off. The first thing you know the devil has slipped a cuss word out of our mouth. That's when we know the Holy Ghost fire needs a stirring up so we can become hot again. That's when we need to exercise temperance and end the conversation, go somewhere and pray in the Spirit, and build up ourselves in the Holy Ghost (Jude 20). We know right then we are losing fellowship with heaven and need to be quickly restored (Psalm 23:3). We start slacking in fellowship with other believers. When we fail to fellowship frequently, we tend to lose a sense of accountability and commitment to our Father and his kingdom.

The Bible says the Body of Christ is one, but many members with the strong helps compensate for the weak. We have to allow ourselves to be open to being helped by each other. "No man is an island."

3) **Not reading the Word of God prayerfully**— Jeremiah 20:9 says, *"...But His word was in my heart as a burning fire shut up in my bones." When we focus on the Word of God, it's hard to become lukewarm.*

Back to the text in Revelation 3:16, and I paraphrase with the RCB (Roger C. Bethel) version: Christianity is not a game for spectators. We have to step up to the plate and swing at the ball or get off the field.

When we stand on the sideline and sell wolf tickets, we confuse the players.

Each team member needs to stay on the Lord's side to hear the commands of his coach, Jesus! When I was a boy, I used to try to play softball. There were always older guys on the sidelines trying to coach players.

Sideline coaches who are not on your team will cause you to lose focus on God. Jesus says I am the only way! It's either his way or the highway. Muhammad can't do it. Buddha can't do it. Even the pope can't do it! Only the one who was raised from the dead is able to keep you hot so you don't become lukewarm or get cold.

Prayer

Father, I thank that your beloved Son, Jesus is our elder brother and seated at your right hand on the throne of grace. We know your grace is sufficient for us to remain hot and not get lukewarm. Thank you for another chance today to get right whatever is wrong with us! Thank you, Jesus, for baptizing us with the Holy Ghost and fire so that we don't become lukewarm. Now, Father, forgive us for our sins as we, right now, purpose in our heart to forgive others. Thank you, Father. Amen!

Supplication

Supplication keeps our head in the door of God's sanctuary.

"Be anxious for nothing, but in everything by prayer and supplication, with thanksgiving, let your requests be made known to God; and the peace of god, which surpasses all understanding, will guard your hearts and minds through Christ Jesus." Philippians 4:6-7 (NJKV)

(Additional recommended scripture reading is Ephesians6:10-18, 2 Corinthians 10:3-5.)

Today's word, "supplication" is a form of communication between mankind and God. Another word for supplication is plead.

Supplication is a manner in which we make a connection with God for a particular purpose or reason. In other words, supplication is a special petition to God according to his will.

"Now this is the confidence that we have in Him, that if we ask anything according to His will, He hears us. And if we know that He hears us, whatever we ask, we know that we have the petitions that we have asked of Him." I John 5:14-15 (NJKV)

Check out Abraham when he supplicated for Sodom and Gomorrah in Genesis 18:16-33. Because God doesn't want anyone to perish but wants all to come to repentance, he honored Abraham's supplication.

Supplication is a type of prayer, but it's more formal than some of the other types, such as the prayer of agreement or the prayer of thanksgiving.

In a sense, supplication is more like the manner in which we approach God with a special request. Again, notice the supplication of Abraham in Genesis 18. I would say supplication is like a special petition that is well thought-out while asking for something major.

One of the best methods to get something big from God is to approach him in a united front, whereby every intercessor is on the same page or in one accord as the believers were in Acts 1:14 (KJV) which says, *"These all continued with one accord in prayer and supplication."*

Here, the believers were prepared and expecting a mighty move from God that was unusual...something new to mankind that they'd never seen.

As a result of their special petitioning they presented to God, in a sense he came down from heaven.

Watch what happens in Acts 2:1. The believers were all with one accord—with one mind, all saying the same thing—in one place in their mind. God, the Holy Spirit, came down from heaven and filled the house where they were sitting. Verse 4 says they were all filled with the Holy Spirit. That's just like my God!

Down through the history of God's relationship with mankind, that was the first time in human history that the Godhead of the universe came down from heaven to actually enter the body of human beings to live and move on the Earth. He would come upon the prophets from time to time but never before had God come to dwell or live in believing human beings.

That was all as a result of the believers' supplications in the upper room making a special petition to God, all on one accord, with one mind, all saying the same thing.

So that's what we as believers in the twenty-first century should be doing on behalf of all mankind.

It goes back to the exhortation to believers in I Timothy 2:1-3 (KJV) which says:

"I exhort therefore, that, first of all, supplications, prayers, intercessions and giving of thanks, be made for all men; For kings and for all that are in authority; that we may lead a quiet and peaceable life in all godliness and honesty. For this is good and acceptable in the sight of God our Savior;"

In conclusion, supplication is what we are doing as we are praying in teams or in small groups. I encourage your first corporate prayer assignment to be a prayer in one accord for our government, then, we want to pray for our children and school system of primary and secondary education.

Prayer

Father, in the name of Jesus, we thank you for your Word that teaches us how to pray and supplicate for your will to be done on Earth as it is in heaven. Amen!

Strength

God will help those who are strong to help bear the infirmities of those who are weak.

"I can do all things through Christ who strengthens me."
Philippians 4:13 (NKJV)

Today's watchword, "strength," is power! (Synonyms – courage, energy, fortitude, stability, vitality, backbone, force, hardiness, potency)

Do you ever get to the point where nothing seems to work out right for you? Then you get spiritually, mentally, and even physically weak. It looks like every way you turn there's an obstacle, and not even your closest friends and relatives understand. They think you're making a mountain out of a mole hill.

That's when we really want to throw-in-the-towel, isn't it? It seems like everybody looks at you sideways or talks about you.

And you know something? That's when we really need to throw in the towel and grab a hold to the horns of the altar. It is at that point, that we have to make up our mind that we will not be moved by what folks say about us. They talked about Jesus, and he was perfect.

When we get weak, emotionally, mentally, and spiritually, we have to remember the power of life over death lies in our tongue. We need to start with the basic principles of prayer: "Our Father in heaven, bless His Name above every other name."

We want to begin to meditate on all his goodness that he does for us through Christ Jesus.

First of all—He forgives all our iniquities. According to God's benefit package found in Psalm 103:3-5:

- He heals all our diseases.
- He redeems our life from destruction.
- He satisfies our mouth so that our strength is renewed like the eagle, so we can run and not be weary, we can walk and not faint. Then we can say like the Apostle Paul in Philippians 4:13 (NJKV), *"I can do all things through Christ who strengthens me."*

In other words, we learn how to get up when we're down. But how many of us really know how to "get up" when we're down?

A lot of times when we get physically down in our bodies, we have a tendency to weaken spiritually, mentally, and emotionally. When that happens, we just don't want to be bothered and give up.

But did you know when an athlete gets weak, he or she gets on a "simple" training regimen to regain their strength:

- They begin with non-strenuous repetitions.

- They keep it simple with better nutrition, proper rest, and lightweight repetitions.

Sometimes we feel pressed down on every side, but we know by the promises of our Father that we are not crushed. Although as stated in 2 Corinthians 4:8-9, (KJV), *"We are troubled on EVERY side, yet not distressed; we are perplexed, but not in despair, persecuted, but not forsaken, cast down, but not destroyed."* This emphasizes what the Apostle Paul experienced spiritually, mentally, emotionally, and physically. But I thank my God, Paul was human just like we are, and we know God is no respecter of persons. Paul knew the source of his strength, and so do we. Hallelujah!

That's how we are able to say as Paul said to the church at Philippi:

"I know how to abound, in other words, I've experienced living high on the hog and I've waded through the mud – I've learned to be full and to be hungry – but I can do all things through Christ who strengthens me." Philippians 4:12-13 (NJKV)

Sometimes when folks who are supposed to love us slap us, it's only natural we don't want to turn the other cheek; or when our relatives take our shirt, we're too spiritually weak to give them a coat, too. But, again, thanks be to our Father, we're more than conquerors through his Son, Jesus Christ, who lives in us by his Holy Spirit. We've got to remember Satan is the accuser of the brethren—God said Job was an upright man with great integrity, and Satan went after him, so you know he's coming after you and me.

Sometimes Satan comes after us before we even get to the mountain we think we can't climb. . . That's called discouragement and is one of his most effective weapons to cut us down, to make us think and say, "I can't do that." But the scripture says, *"I can do all things through Christ who strengthens me."*

I don't think the Apostle Paul was talking about any one type of weakness when he wrote in 2 Corinthians 4:9 (KJV) that *"he was struck down but not destroyed."*

In conclusion, always remember your strength is hardly ever lost all at once! It's usually depleted gradually, so let us make sure we stay close to the source of our strength.

Prayer

Father, in the name of Jesus, help us to internalize that Jesus is the only source of our strength; not our deceased relatives, not the forces of nature, nor our money, good looks, or position in life, but Jesus and him only! Amen!

Testimony

The word of our testimony helps us overcome the three major elements of the world; lust of the flesh, lust of the eyes and the pride of life.

"...For the testimony of Jesus is the spirit of prophecy." Revelation 19:10 (NJKV)

When given in the natural realm, a "testimony" is a written or spoken statement, especially if one is given in a court of law.

From a spiritual perspective, a testimony is the recounting of a religious experience or conversion.

But the testimony of Jesus is his eternal existence from the foundation of the Word to the very end of times—that is, his testimony is eternal—it's the Word of God with all his promises and commandments. It is the good news presented in terms of one's own experience. The testimony of Jesus is the spirit of prophecy.

What is the purpose of our personal testimony from a spiritual perspective? Revelation 12:11 says we overcome the devil by the blood of the Lamb and by the Word or the Jesus in our testimony.

Since we as Christians are disciples or followers and

imitators of Christ, his testimony should be our testimony. So, the scripture says the testimony of Jesus is the spirit of prophecy.

These statements lead us to ask, what is the spirit of prophecy? All we have to do is go back to Revelation 19:10 which gives us the definition that the spirit of prophecy is the testimony of Jesus, from Genesis through Revelation.

In simple terms, the testimony of Jesus is that he is the beginning, the middle, and the end. His name is called the **Word of God**. Scripture tells us that in the beginning was the Word, and the Word became flesh, He was crucified, resurrected, and seated at the right hand of the Father.

What does it mean by the blood and the Word of our testimony? Revelation 19:13 (NKJV) says: *"He was clothed with a robe dipped in blood, and His name is called The Word of God."*

Colossians 1:17 (NIV) tells us: *"He is before all things, and in him all hold together."*

Through these scriptures we can see the importance of our testimony. We overcome the enemy by the Word of God or Jesus in our testimony. The Word, which is Jesus, has no beginning or end.

So we, as believers in Jesus, can call things that have not manifested into the natural as if they have already happened. That's how faith really works. You don't see or experience something and then call it faith. By faith, we call the thing already done before we actually experience it. Hebrews 11:1

(KJV) says *"Now, faith IS the substance of things hoped for, the evidence of things not seen."*

Prayer

Father, I thank you for your Living Word, Jesus, the Christ, who forever lives and is always making intercession for us.

I thank you that Jesus is Lord over my spirit, soul, and body.

Father, I thank you that Jesus is made unto me wisdom and right standing with you.

I thank you that Jesus is the writer of my testimony.

I thank you that I'm redeemed from the curse of Satan. I thank you that we are set apart from the system of Satan.

We thank you that we overcome by the blood of Jesus and the Word of his testimony.

So now I can decree and declare that Jesus is my shepherd, and I shall not want. Because he supplies all my needs. Amen!

Thinking

As we think in our sub-conscious mind, so we act.

"For as he thinks in his heart, so is he." Proverbs 23:7a (NKJV)

Our word for today is a very simple, but profound, word that carries so much weight in human behavior...that word is "thinking."

Too often our feelings outweigh our thinking, and they get us in trouble. But, as Christians, it is important that we work diligently to change our thinking.

So, where do we look to find out how we should think? Good question!

Before we attempt to answer, let's take a brief look at the origin of "thinking." Thinking is a derivative of the soul. That statement demands a lot more in-depth teaching that we will get into later on in our mission to be transformed into God's perfect will.

God wants our souls free to be saved! So, thinking is the main avenue throughout this life journey on Earth.

This foundational scripture is one of the most profound

principles in the Bible that describes what thinking does for human behavior:

"For as he thinks in his heart, so is he." Proverbs 23:7(a) (NKJV)

Thinking is like driving a car. You can't drive but one car at a time. It's utterly impossible for one person to drive two cars at the same time.

That's how thinking operates in human beings. You cannot think spiritually and carnally at the same exact moment. You're either going to think about spiritual things or fleshly things at any given second.

Butting Heads

It's never a pleasant outcome when the Spirit butts head with the flesh. And believe it or not that is possible. Galatians 5:17(NLT) says:

"The sinful nature wants to do evil, which is just the opposite of what the Spirit wants. And the Spirit gives us desires that are the opposite of what the sinful nature desires. These two forces are constantly fighting each other, so you are not free to carry out your good intentions."

As you can see, our wishes are never free from the pressures of these forces fighting to win control over us.

There's as much difference between the flesh and the Spirit as difference between night and day. And we certainly cannot experience both at the same time. Daytime brings light, sunshine, and warmth, while night represents darkness which leads to confusion and chaos because you can't see in the dark. Light reflects the Holy Spirit of God, whereas the other, darkness, represents the enemy to God and his people.

Since correct thinking is a direct offspring of scripture, Philippians 2:5 (NKJV), tells us to: *"Let this mind be in you which was also in Christ Jesus."*

Our mind operates like time on a clock. We can only get one second at a time. Likewise, with our thoughts. We can only have one thought at a time. We cannot think evil and good at the same split second. Sweet and bitter water don't come out of the same fountain. We are either thinking fleshly or spiritually at any given second. Here again, the two mindsets butt heads, because they are contrary to each other.

Double Minded

Here's a good natural example of being double minded. The National Safety Council reports that cell phone use while driving leads to 1.6 million automobile crashes each year. That happens when we try to think on two important things at the same time. The world calls it misplaced priorities.

That proves how hard it to focus on two important things at the same time. Even the Bible tells us in Romans 8:6 (NKJV):

"For to be carnally minded is death; but to be spiritually minded is life and peace."

"A double minded man is unstable in all his ways."

James 1:8 (KJV)

Here's another example of improper thinking. Jacob, the patriarch, called his oldest son, Reuben, "unstable as water" and because of that he shall not succeed. (Genesis 49:4).

When we are inconsistent in our thinking, we'll be inconsistent in words, and our deeds will be unreliable. One minute we are one way, the next minute we're another. It's like pouring water out of a bucket, it's going to follow the contours of the surface.

Our thinking has to be stable in order for our actions to be reliable. When we confine our thoughts to the Word of God, our speech will follow suit. We can then and only then have favor with God and man.

When we think on the power of God to heal as opposed to the symptoms of our bodies, we will speak, *"By whose stripes you were healed."* *I Peter 2:24 (NKJV);* When we think *"Greater is He that is in you than he that is in the world,"* 1 *John 4:4 (KJV),* we begin to realize that *"we are more than conquerors through Him that loved us,"* *Romans 8:37 KJV,* and *"No weapon formed against us shall prosper." (Isaiah 54:17).*

So, we can clearly see that to be carnally minded is to persistently think about things from a worldly point of view. That literally means to base everything on the five senses and not allow the Word of God to factor into your decisions.

To think in this fashion kills everything meant to grow

and produce the fruit of the Spirit in our lives.

Actually, to be carnal minded or consistently thinking on what we feel, see, hear, taste, and touch in the natural leads to defeat and eventually gives the enemy permission to take us out before God is ready for us to die.

That's why it's so critical that we stay spiritually alert. I Peter 5:8 tells us to be sober…that means to keep your head on straight, so to speak, so you can stay vigilant or alert. Why? Because your adversary, the devil, is walking about seeking whom he may devour. That word "may" means to get permission. We automatically give him permission when we think wrong. Remember, "As a man thinks consistently, so is he."

Back in the seventies, I used to watch a television sitcom called "All in the Family." The show's main character was a bigot called Archie Bunker. He had an inappropriate nickname for anybody he disagreed with. His son-in-law, Michael, was called "Meat Head" because Archie didn't agree with his social views. Archie said Michael didn't discriminate against people so he called Michael "Meat Head," implying that he didn't think like him. Someone who lacks depth in thought and action or is shallow-minded always thinks about eating and being merry.

So we need to put forth special efforts to become kingdom-minded and think on whatsoever things that are true, according to Philippians 4:8 (NJKV):

"…whatever things are noble, whatever things are just,

whatever things that are pure, whatever things are lovely, whatever things are of good report, if there is any virtue and if there is anything praiseworthy— meditate on these things."

Some ministers say not to worry about the negative things that cross our minds, that the positive things we think about will override and drive out the negative thinking.

Personally, I think we need to practice keeping our eyes on the prize and drive out negative thinking.

Just as a good driver keeps his eyes on the road and the signs that gives directions, so should the pilgrim on this journey called life stay focused on the Word of God and the light that it gives as we travel along life's highway.

In conclusion, I believe Isaiah 26:3 (NIV) puts this entire message in a nutshell when it says:

"You will keep in perfect peace those whose minds are steadfast, because they trust in You."

We must realize that we are on a journey, so let's keep our eyes on the road. I used to try to drive and sight-see at the same time. My wife would always say in a nice way, "Do you need me to drive?" After several near accidents, I finally learned to stay focused on the task at hand…driving!

Prayer

Let's us pray. Heavenly Father, help us to stay single-minded by keeping our eyes and mind on the prize, our soon-coming Savior, Jesus, the Christ. Help us to think right so we can live right. In Jesus' name. Amen!

Transfiguration

When a subject or object changes form and/or appearance instantaneously before the eyes of the viewer.

"And, behold, there appeared unto them Moses and Elias talking with Him." *Matthew 17:3 (KJV).*

Mystery of the Transfiguration, in its simplest form, is a most profound concept.

Colossians 1:27 (KJV) says: "To whom God would make known what the riches of the Glory of this mystery among the Gentiles is, which is the Christ in you, the Hope of Glory."

As we look at this passage, we have to think about the rich expense of God the Father, Creator of the Heavens, the Earth, and all that dwell within.

Think about how much it cost him to give up his only begotten Son to live within the body of each of us! Thank God for this glorious mystery of the Transfiguration.

"And after six days Jesus taketh Peter, James, and John his brother, and bringeth them up into an high mountain apart,

2 And was transfigured before them: and his face did shine as the sun, and his raiment was white as the light.

3 And, behold, there appeared unto them Moses and

Elias talking with him. Matthew 17:1-3 (KJV)

Transfigured, in the case of Jesus, was an event that temporarily changed his total appearance from a man to a celestial being.

To be **transformed** is to undergo a gradual change in thought patterns behavior, behavior, and character

Transferred is to be relocated from one place to another.

Why did this event, the Transfiguration, take place?

First, let's contrast God's position in the First Covenant with his position in the New Covenant. In the First Covenant, the Spirit of God only made visitations to mankind on Earth. In the New Covenant, God took up permanent residence in earthen vessels.

Who was the Transfiguration to benefit . . . Jesus or his three disciples with him?

First of all, what happened in the Transfiguration?

- The Mountain of Transfiguration was symbolic of God transferring his power and presence to his Son, Jesus.

Moses' appearance and disappearance represented closure to the dispensation of the ceremonial law. The appearance and disappearance of Elijah represented the abolition of God's occasional visitation by the Holy Spirit upon the prophets of God in the Old Testament. In Leviticus 26:12, (KJV), God said to Israel, *"And I will walk among you, and I will be your God, and ye shall be my people."* On the other hand, in the New Testament

God chose to permanently make his residence with mankind by his indwelling Holy Spirit. The evidence is found in I Corinthians 3:16 (KJV) where it says, *"Know ye not that ye are the temple of God, and that the Holy Spirit of God dwelleth in you?"*

The Transfiguration on Mount Sinai represented God taking up a permanent residence on Earth in the heart of mankind.

That is the mystery of Christ in us, the hope of glory that's found in our text of Colossians 1:27b.(KJV).

In conclusion, not only are we as believers being transformed, if we continue in God's Word, we will be transfigured and then, transferred to be in the presence of the Lord for ever and ever.

Prayer

Father God, in the name of Jesus, I thank you for the Transfiguration account in your Word but more importantly, I am grateful for the more sure word of prophecy testified about in II Peter 2:19, that we will do well if we take heed as unto a light that shines in a dark place, until the day dawns and the day star arises in our hearts. Amen!

ABOUT THE AUTHOR

Dr. Bethel resides in Memphis, TN, with Viola, his wife of 36 years. They have five children and 25 grand and great-grandchildren. They serve as Certified Christian Counselors and Therapists. They also host a live intercessory prayer Ministry at 6:55 A.M. CT Monday-Friday at 805-706-5112.

His first professional publication as an independent author is a memoir entitled 'Winning by Default,' a riveting tale about a young boy, the son of Mississippi sharecroppers, who grows into manhood during the "Jim Crow" era. He also co-authored 'Homecoming, Sins of the Father' with Denise Nall.

www.ingramcontent.com/pod-product-compliance
Lightning Source LLC
Chambersburg PA
CBHW022147060526
44654CB00043B/707